A SHOWMAN OF THE BETTING RING

Troubles of a travelling life

JAMES HAZELL

AuthorHouse™ UK
1663 Liberty Drive
Bloomington, IN 47403 USA
www.authorhouse.co.uk
Phone: 0800 047 8203 (Domestic TFN)
+44 1908 723714 (International)

© 2019 James Hazell. All rights reserved.

No part of this book may be reproduced, stored in a retrieval system,
or transmitted by any means without the written permission of the author.

Published by AuthorHouse 06/27/2019

ISBN: 978-1-7283-9012-3 (sc)
ISBN: 978-1-7283-9013-0 (e)

Print information available on the last page.

Any people depicted in stock imagery provided by Getty Images are models,
and such images are being used for illustrative purposes only.
Certain stock imagery © Getty Images.

This book is printed on acid-free paper.

Because of the dynamic nature of the Internet, any web addresses or links contained in this book may have changed since publication and may no longer be valid. The views expressed in this work are solely those of the author and do not necessarily reflect the views of the publisher, and the publisher hereby disclaims any responsibility for them.

authorHOUSE®

ABOUT THE AUTHOR

I grew up in a little village in County Durham. At the age of 6 years old I joined a Traveling show within the betting ring nationwide. My view on life from a very young age has always been to live as though tomorrow doesn't exist, however, this has proven at times to be extremely dangerous and careless, ultimately becoming mentally unable to take care of myself within every day society. I have coasted through the goods times and battled through the bad, however I can now see light at the end of the tunnel. I have the brightest vision within my mind and the strongest message to portray, all in the hope of helping others survive this world that we live in today. My name is James Hazell and this is my story.

PROLOGUE:

Taking a look into my childhood growing up within the bookmaking industry nationwide, the betting ring instantly became my escape from a troubled and unsettled home life. As a child I was moved around a lot, and the trauma which I experienced during my childhood would hold severe consequences in later years. I remember experiencing extreme mixed emotions as a child, it was almost a battle to be loved, and so, when I was presented with the opportunity to join a "travelling show" within the betting ring nationwide, I grabbed it with both hands. I would be aged 6 or 7 years old when I began to attend the races with my Grandad, and I quickly became captured within the jungle that is the betting ring. Some of the other bookies would also take their kids to the races with them, however where they wanted to play in the park at Ripon or go on the Walser at Cartmel, I became enthralled and transfixed by the operation of an on-course bookmaker.

During my early childhood years, I have extremely traumatic memories from within my home life, however I have always faught for more in this life, and I held this fight within me from a very young age!

As a child I was a very happy, outgoing, bubbly soul and even from the age of 6 years old I had become a character within the betting ring. From growing up within the betting ring to establishing myself as a "showman", from the highs of travelling the open world and living life from a backpack, to the lows of dealing with rejection and finding new levels of personal growth within my darkest moments. I personally feel extremely fortunate to have experienced a travelling life of growing up within the horse racing and bookmaking industry, and I now want to share my story with you. So here goes!

CHAPTER 1:
AN EARLY STARTER

"You win the best turned out award kid", some punter stated as I stood before him in my suit and tie. Many of the great characters within the betting ring constantly commented on my ability as a child, I was not like most kids, I would engage in fluent adult conversations and talk all of the business spiel from a very young age. The late old school Scottish bookie Ricky Martin, who was also a dear pal of my Grandad's, gave me the nickname of "wooden heed" as a child. I would attend all of the Scottish horse racing meetings with my Grandad and Ricky, Hamilton was my personal favourite. Many of the biggest characters within the betting ring have nicknames, a few of them are the Rabbit, Bump, Tod Accountant, bonkers, and me, "wooden heed". Life growing up within the betting ring and studying the operation behind an on-course bookmaker, is an education that simply cannot be purchased, everyone within the betting ring becomes a little bookmaking family, personal and financial fuelled feuds are a norm and jokes and jibes a thrown around in banter, I would often be at the centre of a good jibe from the bookies and punters, however I loved the banter and would often reply with a cheeky response.

As we travelled from racecourse to racecourse nationwide, I would constantly sit with my head in-between the car seats, quizzing and questioning my Grandad endlessly about the operation behind bookmaking. I learned to tic-tac the betting show at the early age of 8 years old, however the main form of communication within the betting ring was through walkie talkies. My Grandad would occasionally place me up onto the stool to tic-tac the show for him, just for the show of it I think, and of course I loved it, as I felt a real sense that these stools acted as my platform.

"what price is this favourite James?", Grandad would whisper through the walkie talkie, "9/4 everywhere Grandad", "I've went 5/2 let me know if you spot any 11/4", I could hardly contain my excitement as I floated around the betting ring. I was an extremely well-known figure within the betting ring as a child, so whenever a bookie spotted me lurking around, they knew that something was live!

Grandad would place me up in the grandstands before racing, I'd sit with a Racing Post to hide my face and I'd have my walkie talkie at the ready. It was instilled into me from a very early age to observe the movements of the betting ring, and this allowed me the opportunity of watching the operation unfold live in front of me. I would study how the showmen and women on the betting stools would operate, the immense betting heats unfolding in front of my eyes and I would be dreaming of the day when I could stand up and show off my ability. However, for now, my job was to observe!

The operation behind every bookmaker is different, some will take the more traditional approach by laying the favourite and praying for a result, and others will use a host of various factors and information to form an opinion. I would say that my Grandad is far from traditional when it comes to bookmaking and I would take the same approach by betting to opinion. As a child my Grandad would allocate me a target to follow around the betting ring, observing the inform punters or seeking out information. I would be shoved away from the betting stool "follow him, see what he bets and report back", I buzzed off the adrenalin and very much so felt like a secret agent within the betting ring, taking it all very seriously!

I remember on a few occasions I would be placed onto the front of the joint, my 8 years old self would be shouting in the punters "here on the first event, just make ya way in for a bet", I took to the front man position as though it was meant for me. My time on the front would be cut short by the betting ring manager, one day my Grandad was issued with a £100 fine and I just wanted to be 18 years old so that I could step up to take the betting ring by the balls!

As I was not permitted to take the bets as a child, my Grandad would hand me lumps of cash to sort and count around the back of our pitch. I can remember my thought process as though it was yesterday, I would tell myself "If I can master the art of handling cash and taking bets at the same time, when I'm ready, I will shine within this industry". However, I fully understood from a very early age that to be the best within your profession, you have to dedicate 100% of your time and effort to learn and perfect your trade, and so that is exactly what I set out to do.

There are many roles behind the operation of an on-course bookmaker, however standing up on that betting stool ignited a passion within me like no other! It is the show of it all, you see, as a child, I was always extremely theatrical, in fact I still am today! I would always take on the main roles within the school play and I sang in a choir and sang on a few occasions at our local theatre, however my direction was steered towards the bookmaking and horse racing industry, so obviously I aimed to perfect the major role on the betting stool. I just loved this industry and everything in it, I remember standing in a que for an hour or more at the Knavesmire Racecourse in York, I was queuing to meet Frankie Dettori and to buy a signed copy of his autobiography, I was star struck and in absolute awe of this man and I remember telling myself "I WILL meet him personally one day".

By the age of 10 years old, my life had become extremely unsettled, me and my older brother had been passed through 7 different homes, and through no fault of my own, I simply found it impossible to settle. My school life had become non-existent, I was not interested in learning about pointless subjects, the only things I wanted to learn were odds, percentages, form and techniques on the betting stool. It was during this period within my younger years that I remember sensing a feeling of wanting to escape, I felt as though I needed to get out of my home life, every day became a battle during these younger years! Growing up, I had experienced so many lets downs and so much emotional trauma, that my brain simply could not process the idea of becoming settled into "normal" everyday life. My brother and I were eventually separated, Dale moved in with our Grandma and I moved in with My Dad, his girlfriend Bekki and My younger brother Jake. I was due to start secondary school and I had done extremely well within my SAT exams, meaning I was allocated into top set classes; however, this was not to be my path within my school life.

CHAPTER 2: ESCAPING REALITY

Dale and I quickly settled into life living with Dad and Gran, I shared a room with my younger brother Jake, it was a tiny box room as Dad's and Bekki's house consisted of 2 bedrooms. I had 2 shelves in the closet for my clothes and a few boxes under the bed for my belongings, however I was the happiest I had been in years. It was the summer holidays and I was due to start Comprehensive School in September.

I don't actually remember my first day at big school, however my years there were to be somewhat eventful! I remember finding it difficult to settle in to the top set classes and coping with structure within my school day. Don't get me wrong, I always knew I was an intelligent lad, however my life had never consisted of structure and routine before, and now all of a sudden I had a lot of work to complete, classes to attend and I was even being put down for after school work classes, as that is what comes with being a top set student. However, this was not to be my path during my school life, I very quickly disregarded the idea of myself becoming a top set student, I knew what I wanted to do within my life, or so I thought I did, and that was to have a career within horse racing and the bookmaking industry. The message I want to portrait from this chapter within my life is, no matter what you think you know, always stick in at school and have options behind you, try to think ahead as everything you do during your life holds consequences in future years, no matter what your age.

I wouldn't say that I regret my school years; they really are some of the best memories I have from my childhood and I met some life-long friends. Although my grades and school work had started to slip, I always remained concentrated on my work within the horse racing industry. I would give up every school holiday and weekend to go racing, to learn something new about the trade which I longed for a career in. I remember the first time I attended the Grand National meeting, it is a Thursday, Friday and Saturday meeting, meaning I had to put in a holiday form at school so I could attend, I was so excited! My grandad had bought me a new suit for my birthday, I was quite chubby as a kid so we had to have it altered, however I didn't care, I thought I looked the bee's knees in it and wearing that suit to the races filled me with pride! The Grand National is a stand out meeting of the year for us as Bookmakers, it is extremely high profile and, with thousands of punters attending, it is very much so the show of the year within the horse racing industry. Lots of lights, lots of cameras and lots of action, it was right up my street. This was around the time when I was stopped from working on the racecourse until I was 18 years old, however I carried on working every weekend and school holiday, I taught myself how to do the Betfair and how to control operations from within the office, I never gave up!

School life was beginning to bore me, I did not want to learn about science or how to dissect a frog, all I ever wanted was to go to the races with my Grandad and be on that betting stool, I was really trying to grow before my age, and what comes with boredom for me comes with being irritated and troublesome. I was beginning to get after school detention and exclusion periods almost every week, mostly just for being a cheeky lad or pulling stupid stunts. One day I bought a hamster and I named it Skunky, I took it into school in my backpack and set it loose during an English lesson, the teacher almost had a fit and the whole class roared with laughter, however, looking back, it really wasn't a nice thing to do for my teacher and poor Skunky. What I find when thinking back to my school years is that when I felt as though I didn't fit in, it was best for me to become the class clown rather than to just sit quietly. I was quickly removed from top set classes and placed into the lower sets, which only made me worse.

By now I had formed new friendships both in school and out on the streets. The streets were a place where we hung around as teenagers, we would drink alcohol every Friday night in the woods or under the bridge, I was 12 years old when I began drinking alcohol, and I would say heavily drinking at times. My friend's mam owned a caravan which was parked outside of her house and that's where we first began to party; we call it the caravan days. We would wait around for hours on the street corner, asking adults to go and buy us alcohol from the shop, I used to save up my £2 a day dinner money so that I had enough for 10 tabs and a 2-litre bottle of cider. We would play games of "truth or dare" or "I have never", then, when we were drunk, we would go on midnight missions around the streets waiting for the milk man to deliver his morning milk round so we could pinch a few bottles to cure the morning hangover, it sounds so naughty but it was so much fun at the time. If only I knew how much damage I was causing my future self.

Living with Dad would become a little hectic at times, Jake would be around 3 or 4 years old by now and he was also a lot of hard work. I was also a lot of hard work, when I wasn't skiving from school or getting excluded, I was coming home in a drunken state and spewing up everywhere, it was far from settled.

As a teenager I was a popular kid, a very loud, excitable, boy. My group of friends were amazing, we were a little older and I was settled into school life. We hung around within a large group, some nights there would be around 30 of us in the woods surrounding a camp fire drinking alcohol, the police would constantly chase us or destroy our camps, so we would move on to a new area. We always maintained respect for our village and the people in it, although it was wrong to drink and hang around the streets, we would always do this out of the way of the community, deep in the woods or under the bridge, we built camps to prevent intimidating others. I have a few disturbing memories during my teenage years on the streets, I would experience episodes of rage and anger whilst intoxicated, sometimes so bad that my friends would have to hold me down, as I would be screaming and punching myself in the face. The next day my memory would be a black out, however my friends would record the episodes to show the extent of disturbance within me. Looking back, it was clearly rage and anger projected towards my upbringing, I could never understand why, why does my mam not want to love me? However, shit happens and life goes on.

I was moving into year 9 at school, it was 2006 and I was giving up everything to concentrate on working within the horse racing industry, I was not even making an effort at school, as all I wanted to learn was odds, form, prices, tic tac and Bookmaking, however I held a thought in the back of my mind, "**what am I going to do when I tell people I'm gay**", the stress which surrounded my life from a very young age was unbelievable, but just like everything, and I will say it again, "The show must go on".

My family travel to Thailand each year during the quieter Horse Racing Months, this is something they had been doing throughout most of my life and I was desperate to go with them, looking back, I think I just wanted an escape from reality, an escape from dealing with my life. I pretended to my Grandad that I wanted to travel with him to Thailand for a school report in my Geography class, and I told the school governor's the same spiel so that they would grant me the holiday. In reality, I just wanted to be a million miles away from my life. My Grandad agreed on the holiday, however I had to fund the cost myself and I loved the fact that I could do it. I was working at every opportunity and my Grandad would pay me a pocket money salary, I worked my ass off during the Summer holidays and I managed to cover the cost of the flight and hotel myself. I could not believe it, I was travelling to Thailand, I could hardly sleep with excitement. The mere thought of travelling half way around the world captivated my mind.

I remember my 13 years old self sitting on this huge jet plane waiting to take off, it was my first ever long-haul flight, it blew my mind and that's before we had even departed. I had an image in my head of what Thailand would be like, I knew of the poverty, however the reality of seeing it first hand was some-what different, especially at my young age. We arrived at Suvarnabhumi airport in Bangkok, where we took a taxi to Pattaya which is a coastal city to the east of Thailand. Pattaya is well-known for the seeded night life and sex trade, you would not hear of many 13-year-old children travelling to Pattaya for a holiday, however there I was, and boy what a shock to me little system. "I want to go home, I hate it!", I told my Grandad 5 days into the holiday, the streets of Pattaya are filled with screaming Thai ladies and party goers, "ooh sexy boy, me love you long time", I remember feeling overwhelmed as ladies were pulling and tugging at me to go with them. This one night, I had said to my Grandad "I'm bored and I'm not tired", it was around 9pm and I was not enjoying myself. As I have said before, Grandad is extremely old school within his ways, so he instructed "ooh! you're not tired eh son? put on ya shoes and we'll go for a nice walk", he made me walk with him for about 7 miles all around Pattaya, I remember my feet ached with blisters and he asked "are you tired now son?", I just nodded and went to bed with no arguments.

After a week or so, I began adapting to the Thai way of living and I realised one very important fact of life, "there is more to a book than the cover", in other words Pattaya had a lot more to offer than just the seeded night life. Grandad and I began to adventure out from Pattaya City, we would go to water parks or find remote islands way out to sea, our favourite island is Koh Larn. You can get a boat from Pattaya pier to Koh Larn for 60-baht return, which converted to 80p, as the exchange rate was 70 baht to the pound back then. We called it the "chug-chug boat", as it was so old it would literally chug along the water. We also ventured out on many tourist trips, one particular excursion which I will never forget is the bridge over the river Kwai. We departed Pattaya for 2 nights, we experienced some amazing places which I didn't know existed, such as the railway market, it is the only railway market in the world! All of the local Thai people would set the market up over the tracks, the train would pass through the market at a set time meaning we could stand back to watch the Thai's remove all of the market stalls from the tracks, to allow the train to pass through. We also experienced the infamous Bangkok floating market, before making our way to the river Kwai via the death railway, for an over-night stay. We literally slept on a floating hotel deep into the jungle, it consisted of rafts which were tied together with rope, we showered in the waterfalls and slept in a hammock under the stars, I have experienced nothing like it. Seeing the bridge and the war memorial commemorating soldiers who had lost their lives during World War 2 was extremely tearful, it was named the death railway. Departing Thailand to travel home was extremely testing, as I didn't want to go back to reality.

CHAPTER 3:

BREAKING FREE

I was coming to the end of year 9 in school, the next 2 years would be focused on my GCSE's, however my mind was completely absorbed within my horse racing career and my dream of travelling the world. I would sit day dreaming during my lessons, just thinking about the next time a travelling experience would become available. I had already rebooked to travel to Thailand again the following year, school work had become non-existent for me. It felt as though I had no time for school, even though at 14 I should have had all the time in the world, however I was working in the office at any chance given, planning my career within the horse racing industry and any spare time was spent travelling through to see my Mam in Newcastle. My drinking began to spiral out of control, some mornings I would get intoxicated for school, as I just wanted a reason to be sent home. I hated my life there, I hated that I didn't fit in, all I wanted to do was to go to the racecourse with my Grandad and earn a living.

It was during a science lesson and I had placed a naked flame against the gas tap in the laboratory, I was marched to the head teacher's office, which I didn't fight against, and from that day I never returned back to School. In the end I refused to go to any school for 11 months, I had my life in my vision, I was now working almost every day for my Grandad and saving money for my travels to Thailand, I had also gotten myself a morning paper round, so I was not lying in bed all day during my days off from the office. Here was my 14 years old self, 2 jobs, travelling the world and a bright future ahead of me, I became extremely naïve to the big bad world, as I thought I had everything I wanted. But, at this point, I did.

Not being able to attend the racecourse was really beginning to trouble me, it seemed a lifetime away until I turned 18 and I was so frustrated working from within the office and watching the racing on the tv, however I always gave myself a prep talk, **ya can do this James**. One year, my Grandad appeared on The Morning Line show every morning of the Cheltenham Gold Cup meeting, I had taped it every morning so I could watch him on the TV, I remember wishing that I was stood on the betting stool with him, **I want to be on the TV at Cheltenham**, my dreams and goals were becoming bigger and bigger, I wanted it all. It's funny looking back, once I had been excluded from school and I was working for my Grandad, my alcoholism became grounded, I was planning for my future and for the first time within my childhood I felt a sense of belonging, I felt my place in life.

In 2008, aged 15 years old, I was forced to attend Stanley impact centre, which was a centre for youths who had been excluded from school. I understand that the government holds a duty to house these kids, but with me this was not the best of moves, and I knew it. It was taking me away from a good life and working morals and putting me in a room with naughty kids, what does one expect to happen? Suddenly I went back to trying to fit in, smoking weed and drinking before, and sometimes during the impact centre. Philis, the lady who drove our minibus, collected everyone from their house and one morning I went in legless, and I mean legless! I had consumed a half bottle of whisky, which is seriously dangerous for a 15 years old child. It was the day of my GCSE English, which obviously I failed as I don't think I wrote a single word, actually I think I fell asleep on the desk. Leading up to the end of my school years my Grandad had organized everything for my future before I could blink. I finished education on June 8th 2009 and began full time employment on June 9th 2009. Grandad was going to use the money which I had saved throughout my childhood for a deposit to buy my first home, however, unlike most, Grandad collected me from my last GCSE exam and we drove straight to a meeting with a Barclays mortgage adviser, we were in to buy my first house and the sale was about to go through, I was only 16 years old. It was during this exact time that my feelings for other men became apparent, I had always known my sexuality, but I thought I could hide it, or at least keep it secret, however this would prove to be the toughest next year of my life.

I was in turkey for my last goodbye holiday with Dad and Bekki, the purchase sale for my house had been approved and I was awaiting the keys to move in. During this holiday I was drinking almost every day and going about my business as I pleased, in my eyes if I was old enough to live alone, I was old enough to go out alone and so that's what I did, however this proved to be very dangerous at my young age. I won't give details, but here in Alanya is where I experienced my first sexual experience, I was so drunk and had met some random man in a bar. The next day I woke up with the biggest hangover ever and it hit me what I had done, I was shaking and experiencing panic attacks, yet the worst part of it all was that I couldn't tell anyone, as I was not supposed to be gay. That day, Dad, Bekki and my younger brother Jake booked a trip to a water park, however I shut myself away in the hotel bar, the feeling of shame was immense. I remember the feeling of hating myself, I hated who I was, it was so overwhelming.

Eventually we arrived home from Turkey and I could not wait to move into my new house. I had received the keys and began to buy second hand bits of furniture, I did my best to make my house a cosy home. It really was a blessing at the time, as I had not yet come to terms with my experience in Turkey, the thought of **this is it, I am gay and I can't tell anyone,** was spinning around my mind and I just wanted to be alone. Once the move was complete, it was as though I had placed an adult head onto my shoulders, I knew what I wanted from life, I knew my future destination and I had my plan to become a name within the horseracing industry. My next adventure to Thailand was approaching and this time we had booked for 6 weeks and decided to experience Phuket for the first time. I was approaching 17 years of age and this trip would be some-what different from my previous Thailand experiences.

Christmas 2009 was approaching; I had settled into my new home and was counting down the days to depart for Thailand. I was working almost every day in the office, covering Betfair during race days and completing company accounts when we had no meetings scheduled. In a sense, I was 16 years old but living the life of a middle-aged adult, and I was treated like one too. My friends were enrolling at college or booking group holidays to Ibiza, yet here I was owning my property, completing company accounts, preparing to start back on the racecourses nationwide and travelling the world. I knew I was lucky, but at times I remember the feeling of immense pressure, and I constantly doubted my future within the bookmaking industry due to my sexuality, I still had not come out as gay, **this could end my career, before it has even begun**. Although it was daunting, I just got on with it the same as I did everything else.

Christmas was a little strange this year, the gifts I received consisted of a heated blanket, a pan set and a food hamper, with tins of ham and fruit cake ect., I remember thinking **pass me the slippers and a pipe n am done**. when I told my friends we all laughed about it a lot, Christmas was no longer a time for fancy presents, but a time to celebrate with my family and to be thankful for the things which I already had in my life. Thailand was just around the corner, and if there is one place in the world which I didn't need to worry about being different, about being gay, it was Thailand.

On this occasion, I had booked my own hotel room, I had fell in love with the relaxed atmosphere in Thailand and I was ready to explore my inner self.

we arrived in Bangkok as usual and got our taxi to Pattaya City. Every year we stay in a hotel which is located straight opposite "Boy's Town". I was aware of boy's town from my previous visits but obviously I had never experienced it, as I was a child. Boy's town consists of 2 streets filled with gay bars and clubs, it would resemble a gay scene in England, it is booming with party goers and ladyboy street shows, I was immediately attracted and wanted see what it was all about. In the evening, I would dine with my family until they went to bed, Then I would pretend to go to my room. I would allow 30 minutes to lapse before putting on my party clothes and sneaking out of the hotel. I swear, after a month of doing this the hotel security guards became aware of my motive, they would give me a cheeky wink as I was sneaking back out. I was truly fascinated, everyone was so open, so free, I felt free being here and I could openly share my feelings without the risk of exposure. I frequented one specific bar to the point of becoming a regular and the locals knew my face. Although Thailand is an amazing destination, it is also a country with a dark side. I had become friends with some of the young lads, not much older than myself, who worked within the sex trade. My heart would sink with emotion as they would put up a façade and take to the dance podium. Each worker would be allocated a specific number, which the men whom wished to purchase their services would call out to a waiter. It was usually older men paying for the pleasure of a younger man's company, not necessarily with a sexual motive, sometimes just for their company. Whilst speaking with the Thai workers I became aware it was not a choice but a necessity, their family would require money for food or medicine and their line of work would fund that. Suddenly my problems seemed so small in comparison.

After spending a month in Pattaya I was definitely ready to leave for Phuket, the atmosphere in Pattaya becomes overbearing and I was ready to relax. Experiencing a new destination was exciting, we were situated in Patong Bay and our hotel was located on the beach front. I was staying in the room directly above my family, making it difficult to sneak out at night, however I had become a natural at it. I was uneased by being out in the bars alone in Phuket as I was unfamiliar with my surroundings, I had grown up travelling to Pattaya and the locals would take care of me during my drunken states, whereas in Phuket I would appear vulnerable to the locals. I have always maintained a street-smart mindset whilst travelling, I would perform risk assessments such as "well what if this happened or what if that happened", however one night whilst out for an evening meal I spotted a poster advert for an all-night beach party with DJ David Morals, I was immediately enticed to attend. I had to perform a mission impossible to sneak out, I had said that I was feeling unwell during our evening meal, so we went back to the hotel early, I allowed for an hour to lapse and then I made my move. It was approximately a 2 mile walk along the seafront to the entrance, there was thousands of people and I immediately began to mingle with a group of Australian backpackers. It felt amazing, the sound of the sea whilst raving to a live DJ set, then afterwards we all headed to Bangla road, which is the main party strip in Phuket. Although I was alone, at no point did I feel unsafe however I did not perform my risk assessment well enough that evening! I had run out of money which meant I had to walk back to my hotel, it was approximately 5am and the streets were bare. I was approached by a very tall, broad, ladyboy, "aaaaahhhh you want sucky sucky", I was alone and would appear vulnerable making me a perfect target, however I have many ladyboy friends who have advised me that respect is key, even during a potential mugging, should you ever get into a situation with a Thai, be respectful! I put my hands together in a symbol of respect, "kop kun mac khap, me need to go home to mama and papa" I said politely, however she was not happy at all and began putting her hands into my pockets, I was thinking "yav got no chance me love, I'm skint", however I repeated "no no, kop kun mac khap", which translates as "no, thank you very much" in Thai, and eventually she left me alone. A word of advice to any travellers in Thailand, be respectful of them and they will be of you, if not, fucking run! she was scarily tall and broad.

It was coming to the end of the holiday, we had been in Thailand almost 6 weeks and I had been drinking and partying almost every night. It felt as though I had escaped reality, however I have learned over the years that it is impossible to do, reality is here and time will always pass, face it.

leaving for home was a relief, I love Thailand but it was always good to get back home and settle back into my life. I had a clear picture of who I was now, I was ready to portrait my true self and I was ready to come out gay, **but how? how do I do it?**

Returning to work, living at home alone and paying bills very quickly became all too much, and I was struggling to cope again. I began to drink heavily, I felt it was the only way to cope with my emotions, I used alcohol as a barrier against my feelings. I remember the feeling of suffocation, whether it be with friends, my family or at work, I felt suffocated within myself, I found it difficult to think ahead, the only time I felt a sense of freedom was whilst travelling and so another holiday booking came very shortly. I had booked Salou, the whole holiday experience was alcohol fuelled, I was 17 years old by now and I was tired of living a lie. I had gotten myself so drunk one night and went home with one of the bar workers and the next morning I didn't feel guilty, in that moment I realised I had to tell someone. My friend Julie was the first person to know about my sexuality, again I was extremely intoxicated, but once I had shared my feelings the pressure began to lift. I really could not have cared less for my career at this moment in time, for the past 5 years I had concealed every emotion I felt surrounding my sexuality and now the time had come to live freely within myself.

CHAPTER 4:

THIS IS ME

all of those years spent torturing myself and beating myself up when it actually wasn't that difficult to say out loud, however I struggled with coming out to my family. Like a coward I had asked Dale to inform my Dad and Gran and I told my aunty myself, who gave poor Donna the job of telling my Grandad. Donna has since told me that Grandad replied with "does he need to go to hospital?", you have to know my Grandad to find this funny. I had quit my job though, as I felt like I couldn't deal with the pressure at the time, also my house became unmanageable and the bills were not being paid, I was losing everything I had worked towards but at the same time I was free . . . I was me.

I applied for early release of the compensation money which I had been rewarded as a child for falling down a council manhole, the application was granted and again I planned a get-away. I had planned to meet my friend in Ibiza, I won't bore you with the details, drunken nights, raves in BCM and a coral exploding in my foot whilst fondling in the sea covers it, however my point is that I simply could not settle at home, it never felt like home, I am a traveller, I always have been and I always will be.

I had decided to sell my house at a profit and my move in with my Aunty for a few months. Although I was gutted about losing my home, which I had worked so hard to buy, I also looked on the bright side of life, **the hardest struggle is behind me, I'm accepted now and I have an industry in which I can make something of myself, I will give this my all**. I found another form of escapism within the gay scene in Newcastle, I absolutely loved it! I would finish work and travel through to Newcastle, sometimes not to return for days on end. I was totally abusing alcohol; however, it was disguised so well within my life style that I failed to recognise it myself! One night, me and my friend had been out drinking on the gay scene, we were leaving Powerhouse nightclub at around 5am when a fight broke out. My friend was having some cross words with another lass, this is not unusual in Newcastle at 5am, However suddenly I was being struck across the face by 3 males. I was in utter shock; it was so unprovoked and I immediately dropped to the floor. One of the lads had stamped on the side of my face against the pavement, after I stumbled to my feet, another punched me in the jaw. I remember standing with my mouth wide open as the blood gushed out. The next morning, I woke up with a blurred memory however the pain in my jaw was far from blurred. I took 1 look in the mirror to see a gap had formed between my bottom teeth and I was totally unable to move my mouth. My first thought was not to go to the hospital, in-fact, my first thought was to get to work. It was Cheltenham Gold Cup week and I was covering the in-office activity; I could not let my Grandad down! After I had completed my commitments during the week with a throbbing jaw, I made my way to the hospital and I was immediately rushed to Sunderland Royal Hospital as my Jaw was hanging on by a thread. It was broken in 3 places and required extreme surgery to wire it back together with a metal plate, my only thought at the time was **what about work**, I was that scared to miss out on a single day!

becoming an adult; my life really did evolve when I became an adult, I returned to the betting stool on racecourses nationwide, I was able to travel alone and I could obtain a personal gambling license under my Grandad's Business. My life began to move at 100 miles an hour, I was attending horse racing meetings all over the country in prime betting pitches alongside my Grandad. I had grown up from being a child on the racecourse and the bookies all remembered me, I felt amazing and the betting stool really was my platform. I wanted to be the best worker in the betting ring and so I began to learn and perfect every aspect of the job, from the punters to the horse racing and the techniques on the betting stool. I would practise how to shuffle the money between my fingers, what best ways to hold it, the quickest way to call bets and the quickest way to pay out, day after day until I became the best I could be. I was known for being the "best turned out" worker within the betting ring, ensuring that I was always in a suit, shirt and tie. This was the one area of my life which I had perfected, it was something I loved and I could channel all of my energy into it, **skies the limit**. During 2011 I was sofa surfing with various members of family, until I eventually asked to live with my Grandad, if I wanted to be the best then I had to learn from the best, I had to live and breathe bookmaking and horse racing every single day, and so that is exactly what I did. I settled into my Grandad's house as though it was my own home and for the first time in my life, I felt a sense of belonging.

Towards the end of 2011 my Grandad had earned enough mileage points to claim a free return flight and he chose to travel to Goa, India. My eyes were lit when I heard about the travel and so I had to be a part of it. I asked if I could join and so I did, however, I had to travel alone as we were unable to book onto the same flight, this didn't faze me in the slightest, **get me back out into the world**. I had booked my flight to travel from London and I planned to stay with Josephine the night before as she now lived in London, which was perfect as I had absolutely fell in love with city-life. I flew direct London to Mumbai and I was due to be transferred on to a connecting flight to goa, however I had exited the airport for a cigarette and was unable to re-enter, meaning I had to make my own way to the domestic airport. My heart began to race, I was 18 years old and bewildered by the madness of Mumbai, it was like nothing that I had ever experienced before. I could not think for the noise of cars and bikes, people were trying to get me into their taxis and I didn't know whether to trust them or not, I literally had to sit down and breathe. I told myself **ok, get yaself to a prepaid taxi office,** this way my taxi would be official, I had not even 30 minutes to spare to get to the domestic flight, however I was safe and on my way. Once I arrived, I had a further 2 hours taxi journey from the airport to Baga Beach, it was 1am by now, pitch black dark and I was petrified. I never let go of the car door handle until I arrived at the hotel and finally met my Grandad**. fuck me that was crazy,** but an amazing kind of crazy, the kind of crazy you would want to experience every day. I was sharing a hotel room with my Grandad so there really is no crazy, drunken stories from my Goan adventure, apart from the fact that I had fell in love with India, the culture, the people, the food, it all fascinated me. I met ALOT of people who were backpacking or had travelled India previously and had visited the Taj Mahal. They showed me pictures which captured my mind, I remember thinking to myself **one day James, one day**.

Suddenly, my life became extremely settled, horse racing was the biggest part of my life right now and living with my Grandad meant that I was breathing the passion of bookmaking every day. When we weren't at home watching horseracing and doing accounts, we were on the road attending meetings Nationwide, I considered my job to be a travelling show. Growing up on the racecourse was insightful, getting to know some of the biggest characters within the industry, however I always stood out stood out within the betting ring. The bookmaking industry is predominantly a male dominated industry and I was extremely expressive and some-what camp; however, it was never frowned upon; in-fact punters would take a real shining to me and note my efforts and ability on the betting stool. I remember attending the big festival meetings, such as the Grand National and Cheltenham Gold Cup as a child, however I was yet to experience them as an adult.

Christmas 2011 was an amazing time for me, I felt settled living with my Grandad and I really felt a sense of belonging within my life.

I decided to miss Thailand this year and I stayed at home to help my Aunty run the business. We would be in Scotland one day, then down to Cheltenham the next, we even covered point-to-point racing, which is very old school bookmaking, it really is the best to gain experience. I had been attending point-to-point racing fixtures since the age of 6 years old, I know how to tic-tac the betting show, which for a young, up and coming bookie, is not really the norm our days.

A few months earlier I had sent in an application for the television programme Big Brother, this had always been a dream of mine as a child, and I vowed to myself to follow my dreams as an adult. My best friend recorded the video from my mobile phone, it was a 90 seconds clip of me being extremely hyperactive, I remember how much I loved making that audition clip. A few weeks later, whilst I was working in the office, my phone began to ring, the caller ID was private and a sensation of shivers shot through my body. "Hi, am I speaking with James Hazell, I'm calling from Big Brother, the executive producers absolutely loved your audition video and would like to invite you to Manchester next week for a meeting", my whole body was shaking with excitement, I readily agreed and I was booked in to meet the producers at the Manchester arena. Grandad was not due back home from Thailand until after the audition, and so I didn't tell him anything about the process and off I went to Manchester with my best friend.

CHAPTER 5:
A WANT FOR MORE

I was hanging out of my arse, we had spent the night in a hotel in Newcastle and we had gotten extremely drunk, we over slept the next morning meaning we missed our bus to Manchester and had to pay a fortune for a train fare. Just like every eventuality within my life, this was full of drama, however we finally arrived in Manchester with stinking hangovers. Upon arriving at Manchester Arena my picture was taken and I was handed a sticker displaying my Big Brother auditionee number. The audition process was surreal and I had never wanted anything as much as I wanted this. Once the gruelling audition process had come to an end, I was advised to keep myself available and to await further instruction.

Although I was hung up on the idea that I was going to be a housemate in the Big Brother house that year, my career within the bookmaking industry was moving so fast that, after a month or so, I had put the audition process behind me and became focused on achieving my goals within the bookmaking industry. It was Cheltenham Gold Cup and this was my first festival meeting on the betting stool as an adult, I had been back on-course for almost 1 year now and my performance on the betting stool was improving with each day. Working for my Grandad is far from easy, however becoming the best you can be is never going to be easy, and if there was one thing that I wanted from the betting ring it was to become the best that I could be. Cheltenham gold cup is an extremely high-profile meeting within the horse racing calendar, home to some of the greatest horse racing and sportsman within the industry. What comes with that level of class is one of the greatest shows that horse racing has to offer, and as bookmakers we are part of that show, or at least in my eyes we are. Punters come to the racecourse to gain the full experience, to hear the roaring crowds, to see betting heats filled with punters throwing money at the bookmakers, and as a frontman I had to be able to cope with that. For me though, coping was not good enough, I wanted to excel within my position, and in my Grandads prominent tattersalls position, I had the platform to do just that. I quickly realised that punters would stop to watch me taking bets and the faster I operated, the more punters would spectate. Some punters would stand for hours transfixed with my skills on the betting stool, some would record me and photographers would set up their camera and tripod in-front of me, however, I didn't have time to stop and take much notice, I just got on with taking control of the crowds and my betting heats.

As bookmakers our working year begins with the Cheltenham Festival which takes place in March, from then onwards our racing schedule is back-to-back, attending meetings all over the U.K. As soon as the Cheltenham Festival is over, the planning then begins for the Grand National meeting at Aintree. Grandad held 2 positions at the Grand National fixture, one on the rails and one in main tattersalls, these were 2 very good positions to bet in. I had not attended the Grand National since the days when I was putting in a holiday form at school as a child, and now I was beginning to find my feet within the industry and very much so looking forward to progressing further. Although Cheltenham hosts some of the highest class of jumps racing, the Grand National has always appeared busier, however, the meeting attracts many party goers as appose to racegoers, meaning the cash turnover is usually well below that at Cheltenham. Never the less, The Grand National will always be the "show of the year" within the horse racing calendar. I had begun to develop my own unique shouts on the betting stool which I used to pull in the punters, "hea we go then, on this first event or the Grand National . . take ya pick", as the crowds began to flood into the stands by their thousands, the betting heats are extremely intense and fast-paced at the National, "keep it coming lads, just call em out" . . . " YESS, just shout em out now", I would shout out to the punters as I was taking around 20 or 30 bets a minute. As soon as the race is off, I would ask my computer operator to display the next race and I would open the next betting heat immediately, then as soon as the result is called, the pay-out begins. By now, I had perfected my rhythm on the stool, allowing me to perform the best techniques to ensure the fastest pay-out, so that I could begin to call in the following betting heat. At any one time I could be holding up to £2000 between my left thumb, index and middle finger, with a mixture of £5's, £10's and £20 notes, shuffling them constantly to prevent the notes from sticking together, whilst paying out winning tickets and taking bets, all at the same time. It was 100 miles an hour all day, from morning to night, but I loved it, I would work off the adrenaline. Suddenly, a tv camera appeared in front of me, hovering above the crowds on national day, it was BBC news who were filming me on the betting stool. This was great for advertisement, however, with thousands of hungry punters fighting for a bet, I remember it being quite a hinderance. At the end of each festival meeting I would sit in the car and think **I could do it all over again.**

Between the festival and feature race-day meetings within our calendar, we have what we refer to as mid-week or off meetings, at times we would be on the road for weeks, travelling all over the country with the horse racing. It was not always a glamorous affair, sometimes braving the hailing winds and rain all day, however my Grandad would never miss, "you have to be a hungry fighter in this game" he would inspire. Months would pass by quicker than ever, always at a pace we could hardly keep up with, but somehow did. From the Scottish Grand National to Perth Gold Cup, Ladies Days, Cumberland Bell, Northumberland Plate, Ayr Gold Cup, and everything between, it was constant. My Grandad held pitches 1, 3 and 8 on the rails at Newcastle Flat and the highlight of the year is the Northumberland Plate. My Grandad had clearly recognised my potential on the betting stool as each day he would position me on the best pitch. A family friend Jane Ridley, Daughter of the high-profile northern bookie Johnny Ridley, had brought a racing magazine from their betting shop, which featured an article on fractional odds. Here I was pictured at the Cheltenham Festival, the photo had been selected for the article, I remember feeling so proud and thanking Janey for keeping the magazine for me.

Only a matter of weeks after the Northumberland plate meeting comes the Newcastle's Ladies day event, although the class of horse racing is left to be desired, the crowds come out in their thousands and it is one of the more glamorous days within my calendar, as the sun always shines over Gosforth Park on Ladies Day. Ladies day 2012 sticks out in my memory, I was betting away on the front of No.1 pitch on the rails, as always, I was working the crowds and pulling in the punters with a bit cheeky banter when a producer from Geordie Shore approached me. "we are looking to bring the Geordie Shore cast into the betting ring to place some bets, we have watched you working for a while and you'd be great", although I didn't even watch Geordie Shore I agreed, it was all free advertisement and publicity for the business. The cameras began to set up and they positioned themselves to the side of my pitch, we filmed for about 20 minutes with the cast and then I got on with my work.

During this point within my life horse racing and travelling consumed almost all of my time, I had booked to go to Thailand in January again, it had been 2 years since my last trip to Thailand and I had grown up so much within those 2 years. I was also taking my driving lessons with the aim of passing my test, buying a car and representing my Grandad's business nationwide, I was completely focused on achieving my goals. The betting ring had become my office, and boy what an office it was, filled with some of the greatest characters I have ever met. Most of the larger than life characters within the betting ring have nicknames, such as "rabbit" a man who I have known all of my life, he helped to teach me the game! he'd greet me with a slow voice "now then James, how's that diary looking, any spare days for ya old pal". Grandad had handed over control of the staffing to me, and I would always pencil in Rabbit where I could. The knowledge, tales and banter which he possessed within the betting ring simply could not be purchased.

I would be counting down the days to the Cheltenham November festival. I would name Cheltenham as my all-time favourite racecourse within the UK for many reasons, but one particular reason is the hair-raising shivers of excitement you feel when walking into the betting ring. The immense size of the racecourse and seeing it completely bare at 9am whilst setting up our equipment, knowing that in a matter of hours it will be shoulder to shoulder with roaring punters, gave me a thrill which I would constantly crave. I began to take note of the same familiar faces whom placed their bets with me, the same punters would be watching from the grandstand in front of our pitch, it would entice me to work harder, shout louder and take bets faster, knowing that the punters actually wanted to see this. I remember glancing up to the stands above me to see punters leaning over to watch my bet taking skills on the stool, **this is the reason I do what I do**, as much as I love the horse racing, my true passion has always been for the crowds and the show of it all. As soon as Cheltenham is over, our year begins to wind down and we look forward to a month holiday in Thailand.

CHAPTER 6:
FORMING AN ALLIANCE

Travelling to Thailand had become a norm within my life by now, however this year I would form an alliance with another bookie, Rebecca Clarke. Although I had made acquaintance with Rebecca on course over the years, our paths had never crossed on a personal level as our career paths operated on a completely different scale. I remember our first night out together, we must have sat for 5 hours sharing stories of growing up on the racecourse, in-fact we sat for so long our bar bill was almost 3000 baht, which is a fortune in the sailor bar. I could immediately identify with Rebecca's love and passion for bookmaking and horse racing, it was just as strong as mine and, what's more, we had a bond, we clicked immediately. I remember thinking to myself **when I become a representative for my Grandad's business, she will be my number one worker**, she ticked all of the right boxes, she possessed a broad knowledge of the game, she could drive and she was a bookie herself with a gambling license. I had my plan and I was ready to implement it.

Another memory in Thailand springs to mind, I had met a Russian man in boy's town, I was young and single and he was hot, so I went to the nightclub with him. He had asked me back to his room, I know how dangerous this sort of behaviour can be, however I was extremely naive to the big bad world and so off we went on his moped. He took me to a cul-de-sac of apartments where we received a key from the concierge at the main entrance, I began to get a little apprehensive at this point, yet still I went with it. When we got into the apartment, it was what I can only describe as a sex room, I shit you not! This was something you would only see in a movie. There were mirrors on each wall and on the ceiling above the bed, there was a basket with an array of pleasuring gels, condoms and a sex chair with leg holders, 50 shades wouldn't have a look in! obviously nothing happened between us, otherwise I wouldn't be telling this story, I put a stop to it thinking **what if cameras are behind the mirrors**, or even worse people watching, you just never do know in Thailand. The advice from this story would be not to go off with strangers, and if you do, make god damn sure it is not to a sex bungalow in Thailand!

Once we return home from Thailand, life on the road starts again with preparation for the Cheltenham Gold Cup. I had been approved my personal gambling license by the gambling commission to operate under my Grandad's business, I only needed to pass my driving test to begin representing Nationwide. I remember the morning of my driving test, I was totally confident and needless to say I passed with only 4 minors, **get in, now the fun begins**. It was also my 20th Birthday the same month, it literally felt as though I had grown from a teenager to an adult there and then. I was insured on the company car the very same day that I passed my driving test and I immediately started to rearrange the racing diary as I became head representative for Byan D Hazell Racing nationwide. The very first decision I made within my new role as representative was to appoint Rebecca as my business partner nationwide, she obviously agreed and I began to schedule her into the diary on a weekly basis. I remember our first day on the betting stool together, it was at Ffos Las in south wales, we usually stayed overnight at Tewkesbury to break up the journey.

Ffos las is one of the many betting rings which has caused extreme controversy over the recent years, due to the compressed SP returns. This is more than likely due to on-course bookmakers collectively agreeing to work to a percentage per horse, in order to cultivate an expandable margin for financial gain. Now, obviously on-course bookmakers have to make certain adjustments within their operation to move forwards with the times and just like any other industry, we also have to adjust accordingly to make it fit. However, a number of betting rings nationwide have taken this collective agreement and abused it, I personally think it disgusting that a horse which should be priced at 50/1 (example) is returned at 16/1 (Example) SP. However, this is the world that we live in today #gluttony, what was originally an agreement between on-course bookies to work to a percentage, has been abused so severely by certain betting rings out of pure greed, that it has caused a great amount of controversy within the industry and investigations have formed within certain betting rings to monitor this.

My grandad had taught me everything he knew about the trade, he provided me with the platform to become an individual within the industry. He gave me sound advice all of the time, however, one particular piece of advice which springs to mind is "they will all appear to be your friend, but given the chance they will stab you in the back, this is a cut-throat industry son, always remember that".

I would begin my day by purchasing a racing post, we would always go for something to eat in the stable lad's canteen before racing so I could study the card. I would listen intently to the surrounding conversations, picking up any pieces of information that was of value to my operation, or even recognising the stable staff in-case they placed thier bets in the betting ring. The stable lad's canteen is a cafe were all of the horseracing staff eat, stable workers are usually the folk to watch for useful information, monitoring which horses they back. Then, I would phone the office to monitor the early prices from the exchanges to provide an indication of the market fluctuation. I would generally mark up my own card, using my various research methods and marking the form of each runner to help mould my judgement on the betting stool. As Bookmakers, there's so many different aspects to take into account before stepping up on to the betting stool, and I wanted to perfect each and every one. I would also ask for Rebecca's opinion, I would ask her to give me a horse which she did not fancy from the card and I would make it a loser, this would give her a sense that she was my business partner. Now, that was our relationship within the betting ring, however we were 2 young, inspiring bookies who shared the same interests in life, and one thing which we both loved to do was to get dolled up for a night out on the town. We would always plan a night out together whilst we were on the road, most of the time it would be in Cheltenham, or if we were travelling from South to North we would book a night in Blackpool. We totally loved our lives, we loved our jobs and I thought I was set for the rest of my life.

CHAPTER 7:

RECOGNITION

My life has always been lived at 100 miles an hour, the pace was manic, however I was taking it all within my stride, working endlessly to achieve my goals. Whenever I achieved one goal, I would set another, and now I had achieved so much within such a short space of time, I found myself wanting more from the industry. My pictures were beginning to pop up in betting magazines or newspaper articles on a regular basis, and I appeared to have quite a strong on-course following. Whenever I stepped up onto the betting stool, whether it be at Newcastle, Ayr, Cheltenham or Ffos Las, punters recognised who I was and they wanted to bet with me, and I loved it! it made me burst with pride to know my job was bringing people back to the races. One particular punter which I had formed a connection with was a lad named Domonic, Dom has difficulties and his speach is badly affected, I don't know much about his condition, however I do know he suffers with communication problems. His mam and dad take him to the races regularly and he struck a chord whilst placing a bet with me. No matter how busy I was, I would stop what I was doing to allow for Dom to place his bet himself, in his own time. He loved to give me the money to place the bet himself, "good luck Dom" I would say, and I would give him a pat on the shoulder. As time went on, Dom was attending meetings every week, seeing how his face lit up when he placed a bet with me really tugged on my emotions, as he was walking away, he would give himself a pat on the same shoulder that I had patted him a good luck on, I came to realise that this was his way of saying thank you. This was the reason I loved my job so much, seeing how happy Dominic was whilst coming to the races with his dad always brightened up my day.

I was busy working away at Cheltenham when Tanya Stevenson approached the joint to speak with my Grandad, I was aware that Tanya was a channel 4 racing presenter, however I never got myself involved within my Grandads conversations unless invited to do so. My grandad would speak with many high-profile figures within the industry, so this was no different, I just kept my head down and got on with my work. It was only when I spotted Tanya and her team during the betting heats, they were stood opposite watching intently whilst I worked away on the betting stool, however, I would have hundreds of people in front of my pitch at any one time and my main priority was to keep control of the betting heats, because if I crumble as a front man, then the crowd becomes frustrated and the whole operation loses its momentum. I had no time to think about it until I was in the car on the way home. Scenarios were spinning around my mind, **why was she watching me? I'm just a 20 years old worker,** and trust me, in the bookmaking industry 20 years old workers, or any workers for that matter, just do not attract that sort of attention. I mentioned it to my Grandad on the journey home, however it was brushed aside and so I just forgot about it.

2014 was quickly approaching, Rebecca and I had formed a solid friendship both On-course and off, and I was making a profit on the betting stool. We had booked to travel to Thailand together, it was the first time we had booked a trip to Thailand without the parents, and we could not wait. We represented at Cheltenham on New Year's Day and then we flew from London Heathrow to Bangkok the very same evening, it was the perfect way to begin 2014. We had only booked for 13 nights, as my Grandad had delegated the running of the business to me whilst he enjoyed 6 weeks Holiday himself. I remember thinking to myself **if Rebecca and I can manage a holiday together, and she can put up with my antics, then I have found a friend for life,** trust me I'm not easy to deal with at times. Travelling is a true testament of a relationship, it either makes you or brakes you. The holiday could not of went any better, filled with island visits, water parks and lots of partying, it was truly amazing.

As soon as we returned home, we dived straight back into our work schedule head first, from Newcastle, to Ffos Las, to Doncaster, to Musselburgh, it was full steam ahead and I was making it profitable on the betting stool. The game of bookmaking can be amazing and it's great when your winning, but when you start losing you have to maintain the mind-set of a saint to keep on track, "never chase your losses, leave the last race behind you and concentrate on the next", this is what my Grandad always taught me. It was Cheltenham trials day and I was betting in pitch 4 on the rails, a prime pitch to bet in and so I give it my 110%. I remembered this day clearly as I had spotted Tanya Stevenson in the stands and she was alongside the legend that is John McCririck, he is such an empowering figure within the production of horse racing. Once again, I had attracted the attention of Tanya, only this time she approached me, "how's business for you today?". When she returned to the stand, I noticed that I was the topic of conversation with her associates, it was these very moments that boosted my performance on the betting stool, it kept me focused on being the best that I could be.

CHAPTER 8:
A LONE TRAVELLER

It was approaching my 21st birthday and I wanted to celebrate it in style, so I decided to use the money which I received in gifts to pay for a Mediterranean cruise. I had always dreamt of going on a cruise with no expense spared, balcony cabin, upgraded room and all the excursions. I decided upon the Ventura fly by cruise from Venice, I wanted to guarantee the weather so I booked for mid-August, I was so excited. I had been dating a lad at the time, it was my first relationship and I thought that I was in love, head over heels in fact, and I initially booked the cruise with him. I have always been the kind of person to treat others with my success, I had paid friends on countless holidays and weekends away, and within this relationship I was funding almost everything we did together, however I was blinded by affection. I'm not going to lie, I do have massive issues surrounding trust and affection, it is more than likely to do with my childhood, however, I am also an extremely strong minded, independent lad and so I planned to go on the cruise alone. After all, I had paid for it out of my birthday money and why should anyone miss out on something so special because of a brake-up, **let's do this**. I had made the decision to go alone, it would not have felt right to go with someone else when it was planned to be a romantic get-away, however, I was an experienced traveller by now and although I was shitting myself due to this being my first adventure alone, I was also on cloud 9 at the thought of it.

I could not afford to take more time off work during the busy summer months, so I had to work at Ripon races all day and then drive to Manchester ready to depart for my cruise. I had packed my best attire, and I was ready for a thrilling adventure, I immediately realised **this ain't gunna be all that bad**. With a cruising holiday you become a cruising family, all of the passengers on board the flight were guests on my ship, and I never even had to worry my mind about the travel, you are transported from one destination to another with no worries. After quite a long day's travelling, I arrived to the ship, standing in awe of the sheer size of it! After checking-in on board and receiving my itinerary for the week, I was guided to my room where my suitcase had been ported straight from the plane to outside my cabin door, I felt like a prince. The room, I mean omg the room, it exceeded my expectations, everyone had joked "eeee you'll be stuck in a cabin under the sea, unable to breathe", this definitely was not the case. The first night on board is a black-tie captains welcome drink, I put on my best attire and headed down to the lobby, however I quickly snuck away. It wasn't really my scene, everyone was in tuxedos and ballgowns, there was a red carpet, champagne and propped paparazzi to snap your welcome pictures. I was desperate to explore the ship, it resembled a shopping mall on the sea consisting of several bars, a theatre, a show room, a casino and several restaurants, it even had a nightclub. The top deck included 4 swimming pools, a gym, fitness suite and more bars and of course the all-day buffet. I was chaperoned to my table for the evening meal, it is amazing how personal they are with your booking, I had stated that I was travelling alone and so I was allocated a table with other single travellers, I felt at ease whilst fine dining with my fellow cruisers. When dining in the al a carte restaurant you are seated with the same people every evening, so they become your dining family. If anyone is feeling alone and experience thoughts of "why am I missing out on life", take the first step and book a cruise, you will never feel alone and there is something for everybody; I mean I was 21 years old and having a blast. If you are a foody person like me, then a cruise would feel like all of your Christmas dinners at once, a 3 course al a carte meal in a gourmet restaurant, an all-day luxury buffet and anytime room service, all included. Here I was, sipping cocktails whilst watching cabaret on the finest of ships, somebody could have told me that I was dreaming and I would have believed them.

I had spent months researching the different tourist attraction in each port. The first Stop was Venice, I had always dreamt of dining in St. Mark's Square and when I arrived it was more than I had imagined. Venice is a city like no other, with gondolas (long boats) used as transport, it is literally the city built on water. The architecture in Italy is breathtakingly beautiful, however should you wish to dine in St. Mark's square, be prepared to pay. I found the most idyllic spot outside a local bistro, I dined outside with an amazing view of the square whilst being serenaded by a violinist. I ordered a ham croissant and a small glass of red wine and I almost choked at the bill of 26 euro, but you really do get what you pay for within the surroundings. Upon departing Venice, we spent a day cruising out at sea, I immediately began to attract some attention from the other passengers as they were curious as to why I was travelling alone, for me the best part about travelling is sharing our adventures. It was karaoke night on the ship and I performed my "all that jazz" routine, this is by far my favourite karaoke song and the whole room stood to their feet in applause, it felt amazing. The ship then arrived in Rome, although I had originally booked an excursion to see the Colosseum, I had slept in due to way too many cocktails the night before, so I packed my backpack and headed out on my own little adventure. I had to take the local train and use a map to find my way, however I eventually made it to Vatican-city, which is the most famous attraction in Rome as it is home to the pope. Having done my research of each port before I left, I was most looking forward to visiting Montenegro, which really is a hidden gem within the Mediterranean. When the ship cruised into the port of Montenegro, we were surrounded by the mountains above us, the ship rotated into port whilst everyone stood in awe on top deck, the sun was blazing and the mountains were literally rotating around us, it was stunning. I had set my sights on the highest point in the port and so I set out on my adventure to climb to the peak of the black mountains. it was thousands of steps up, however upon reaching the summit the views were breath taking, I would strongly recommend Montenegro as a must-see destination. The cruise was coming to an end and I was preparing myself to return home, back to the madness that my life had become. Grandad had appointed me as co-director of Dale James Bookmakers LTD. and I desperately wanted to prove my worth within the industry.

CHAPTER 9:
"YOUR BOY IS SPECIAL ON THAT BETTING STOOL"

Grandad had received a phone call from John McCririck, John had personally phoned my Grandad to praise my ability on the betting stool, "your boy is something else when he is up on that stool mind" he had stated. When grandad told me, I could hardly believe it, however I took my mind back to when I spotted John and Tanya observing my performance on the betting stool on Trials day at Cheltenham earlier in the year, I was overjoyed. The Cheltenham November festival was upon us, and all of the positive feedback which I had gained from high-profile figures within the horse racing and bookmaking industry pushed me further towards my goal, **work harder** I told myself. No matter what meeting I attended, whether it be Cheltenham Festival or Sedgefield off, I would dress to impress. This was my image and I wanted to portrait myself as the best, so I had to give my best within every aspect of my job.

I was on the stool betting away at Cheltenham and as I glanced up a gentlemen was stood in front of the joint trying to take a good picture of me on his phone, I had spotted this particular character around the betting ring with Tanya Stevenson, and so, I paused to allow him to take his snap, "did ya get a good'n" I cheekily laughed and I thought no more about it, until a few weeks later when I was shown the online article which featured the photograph. I now know that the man who had taken the photo was Simon Nott, a huge figure within bookmaking publications and a free-lance writer/blogger of "tales from the betting ring". Simon had featured myself and Gregory Hughes in the article and the photo of myself has the caption "but even Greg was no match for Bryan Hazell's Grandson, the champion bet taker of the meeting". I literally punched the sky in joy, it is articles like this that any bookmaker would want to feature in, let alone a 21 years old worker, I could clearly see my progress within the industry. I was no longer considered as just a worker, but as a figure within the betting ring under my own name, praised for my ability on the betting stool and outdoing my rivals, such as one of the biggest high-profile Irish bookies, Gregory Hughes.

I had a few more travelling adventures in the coming months, including 2 trips to Thailand, so I had decided to take on a late-night bar job alongside my racing work to help fund my travelling escapades. Some days I would go out to work at the races from 7am and return home to go back out to work behind the bars in Consett until the early hours. I remember Brian Clarke telling me "James, you are burning the candle at both ends and eventually you will burn yourself out", but I felt fine and I was earning a decent weekly wage.

It was winter 2014 and our horse racing meetings were beginning to die down, so I decided to take on more shifts behind the bar. I was planning so many adventures for 2015, I could barely keep up with myself. 4 days before Christmas I had been out to work at Newcastle races and came home to work behind the bar, this was my last shift before the festivities and the bar staff decided to stay behind for a few Christmas drinks. I had my car with me and I didn't really feel too intoxicated so I decided to drive, a pathetic and totally irresponsible decision. My car was a large Mercedes estate and, at the time, it had a spare tire on. Suddenly I had lost control of the car, the road conditions were awful and I crashed into a tree. I sat in complete shock, I knew that I would be over the legal limit of alcohol to drive, however, I waited for the police to arrive as I did not want to chance making off from the scene and causing myself further trouble. I was taken to Durham police station and, as I predicted, I was over the limit and about to lose my driving license, **shit!** Everything I had worked for was about to crumble, however I had to keep it together. In the end, I received a driving ban of 36 months from the courts and my car was written off the road. I was utterly ashamed and disappointed within myself that I had allowed this to happen, and my Grandad gave me one hell of a telling off too. However, I had a lot of support within the bookmaking industry, workers and family members who were willing to drive for me, so it didn't cause to much stress within my working life, however it completely took away my independence within my career.

Rebecca and I had booked to travel to Thailand together for the New Year Celebrations, and we were staying at the Ibis river in Bangkok to see in the new year 2015. We watched the fireworks display by the riverside, which was absolutely breath-taking, and then we partied on Koh San Road until the early hours, in fact Rebecca had to escort me back to our hotel room using a luggage trolley, as I was too drunk to walk myself. We departed Bangkok on New Year's Day for our yearly holiday in Pattaya. Rebecca has been travelling to Pattaya since being a child and this would be my 8th or 9th visit, so we were familiar with all of the locals, they had watched us grow into young adults each year, it really was a home from home. I was beating myself up the whole holiday at the fact that I had lost my driving license, "what am I going to do Rebecca", I simply could not get over the trouble that I had caused for myself. For me, what comes with stress and worry comes with alcoholism, it has always been the only coping mechanism that I have known, and so I hit the drink hard in Pattaya. One-night I was out alone in boy's town, I had arranged to meet Rebecca at evening for our nightly meal outing, however I had gotten myself into a right state. "2500 baht, we want 2500 baht" the Thai workers in the bar were screaming at me. I did not run up a bill of that amount so I was refusing to pay, I didn't even recognise some of the items on the bill and I was aware from previous experience that this is a con some bars will try when they see that drunk tourists are alone, in an attempt to swindle some money out of them. Suddenly a Thai worker came running out from behind the bar with a machete knife, I jumped up and I ran out into the street screaming and crying. He held the knife to my throat and he was screaming at me in Thai, I couldn't understand him but I thought my life was going to end and I began to have a panic attack. I could not breathe for crying and screaming, nobody even came near to get involved, however I suppose you would be apprehensive to do so with a crazy Thai man holding a machete in his hand. The tourist police eventually arrived and I explained to them that this was not my bar bill, they explained to me "listen, the best thing you can do here is to pay the bill and leave". They transported me back to my hotel so that I could obtain the cash from our hotel safe. I remember breaking down when Rebecca opened the hotel door, I've never hugged someone so tight in my life! Luckily enough we were due to depart Pattaya to head for Bangkok and Hua Hin, thank god!

We decided to treat ourselves to a night in the luxurious Shangri La hotel in Bangkok for a one-night stay, we were totally in awe of our surroundings. Upon arriving we were ported to our hotel room and it was unbelievable, we were around 15 floors up with a room overlooking the river, that evening we watched a firework display whilst enjoying a beverage from the mini bar, **someone pinch me please, I'm dreaming**. That night we met up with the Emirates cabin crew as Rebecca is good friends with one of the crew members, however this night I steered clear of getting drunk, I think I was still reeling in shock from the events in Pattaya. We travelled to Hua Hin for our last few nights in Thailand before heading home, as I had to run the business.

I found it particularly difficult this year to perform my representative duties, as I had to rely on other people to transport me to and from the racecourses nationwide. My Grandad had always taught me "think of the operation like a chain, once there becomes a weak link in the chain, it brakes", with me not being able to drive, I had become the weak link and it was beginning to cause huge amounts of stress and pressure within my every day. I had quit working behind the bars and decided to focus every ounce of my energy into promoting myself and my Grandads business within the industry. With the Cheltenham Gold Cup approaching, I was set on performing to the best of my ability on the betting stool.

Arriving at Cheltenham is always amazing, I plan the 4 day meeting months in advance, which outfits I will plan to wear, from the hats, to the shoes, coats and scafes, my Grandad would always say "bah lad, yav got more gear than enough", it literally would be packed up to the roof of the car. Walking into Cheltenham Racecourse early morning is breath-taking, seeing the empty stands and appreciating the full view of the course. By now, Grandad would leave me to bet alone whilst he went off to get all of his markings and do his research for the day, I loved it. We bet in pitch 6 at Cheltenham, which meant we could arrive at 9am and begin to set up ready for the gates opening to the public at 10.30am. I wanted to be the best, whether it be from pitch six or pitch one, I would use everything to my advantage. John Hughes, a high profile Irish Bookmaker, held pick 1 in main tattersalls at Cheltenham Festival, however, I would make sure that I was set up and the board was priced before his team even arrived on-course, as they made their way to the number 1 pick I would start with my shouts "hea get on early lads, on the first event or the gold cup". Once the gates open to the public, the punters begin to flood in to the tattersalls betting ring and it is imperatively important to have the prices on the board at this time, so that I can begin to pull them in for a bet. The days working at a feature festival, such as the Cheltenham Gold Cup, are gruelling, from 9am through to 6pm of constant bet taking and pay outs. The betting heats are unbelievable, men and women climbing on each-others back just waving money around, and it is my job to keep control of the heats, not only that, but to excel and take bets at a pace that nobody else could keep up with. I would attract a lot of on-course attention from punters who would stand recording me in action, they would stop to ask "how do you keep up with that", as I am ramming bets through at 100 miles an hour and paying out at the same time. My operation on the betting stool is something that I have perfected over many years, and I have mastered the profession of taking bets at this level. Sometimes you would get a punter walking up with a bag of perhaps £5,000 or £10,000, and you are expected to count each note before issuing the bet, and of course you have to be quick. At the level to which I work towards if even one small error occurs within my operation it would slow my whole performance down, there is no time for mistakes. I have become a diva during stressful mid-betting heats, pulling out the plugs in frustration.

CHAPTER 10:
"THE SHOWMAN OF THE BETTING RING"

It was Day 4 of the festival, which is the Cheltenham Gold Cup day 2015. I was transporting our equipment into the track at around 9am that morning, however I decided to walk around by the parade ring entrance into the course. This entrance passes by all of the makeshift studios for the television teams, including channel4 racing. As luck would have it, at the exact time I was passing by, Tanya Stevenson stepped out from her vehicle. I stopped to speak with her briefly and she asked "can we come over to bother you with the cameras during racing", of course I agreed and I immediately began to prepare myself for the interview. This was set to be a feature interview from within the betting ring on channel4 racings main show on the biggest race-day of the year, I knew that only a selection of bookies had previously gained the opportunity to appear in such an interview, and I was overwhelmed at the fact that I had secured it with Tanya. As the cameras made their way over to our pitch, I expected for them to aim towards my Grandad for the opening interview piece, he is the bookie after all, however Tanya opened the interview with me. "I am here with one of the great showman of the betting ring, James Hazell", the crowds were gathered around the joint and I began to speak naturally, talking about the first event, the horses of interest and the feature race of the day, the Gold Cup. I stated "the crowds are beginning to gather and the show is well on its way", to which the punters around the joint let off a huge roar. The interview passed over to my Grandad to be tied up. As soon as the lights went down and the cameras went off one of the head men with Tanya Gave me a nod of approval as he praised "well done". I jumped down from the betting stool and thanked Tanya, "thank you so much", I felt euphoric and I was lit with adrenalin, "we'll be seeing you at Newcastle James" Tanya stated, and I could hardly believe it. I was only 21 years old and this was something huge for someone my age.

As soon as I was in the car travelling home I switched on my mobile phone to see an array of positive messages, online forums and twitter punters quoted " a master of his own art", it sent butterflies to my stomach and I wanted to relive the whole moment again, and so I retrieved Tanya's phone number and txt her thanking her, she had made that festival so special for me. I later found out that the cameras had rolled over to Clare Balding who commented on the style in which I was shuffling the money between my fingers, this was the icing on a very large cake for me. As soon as the madness of one festival is over, we are back on the road and working all of our mid-week/off racing meetings. The first meeting we attended after my appearance on Channel4 Racing was Carlisle Races. There is a well-known saying in the betting ring which comes from the Yorkshire bookies which springs to mind, "av got ring bah balls lad", this translates to, "I have got the betting ring by the balls", meaning I am in control of the betting ring, and that day my pitch was very much so in control. We were betting in maybes pitch 7 or 8 along the line, however, out of the few thousand punters that were attending that day the majority came to me for a bet, congratulating me on the interview and asking for a photo. I could see the prime pitch bookies in pitches 1&2 looking across in frustration, this was advertisement for the business and at no cost, well, other than me putting every ounce of energy into my performance.

I had booked to go to Paris the next day, I was exhausted after working a hectic week at Cheltenham and racing over the weekend, so I could not wait. I was going alone and I did not care, although I had previously experienced my cruise alone, this was the first time I was travelling with no set plan or itinerary, just my own adventurous mind. Claire dropped me at the airport and off I went. I had always dreamt of Paris, I wanted to experience it all, champagne at the top of the Eiffel tower, Siene river cruise, gourmet meal in the moulin rouge show house and Disneyland Paris. I had a map of Paris and I was set to go. During this trip my favourite memory was that of the moulin rouge show, I had a front row table and it was spectacular, it is another one of my highly recommended attractions to visit. I had always dreamt of dining at a corner cafe with one of those red and white tartan table clothes (like you see in the movies), eating cheese, sipping red wine and reading Cheryl Cole's autobiography, and here I was just taking it all in. My home life had become chaotic and as much as I loved it, I had to break away at times to just zone out, and travelling the world was becoming one of my biggest dreams. When I arrived home from Paris, I decided that I was now able to travel alone into the open world, and so I booked my dream travel, India north to south. I started to plan the adventure and I would leave the day after the Cheltenham November Festival. I had booked a really cheap flight from London to Mumbai for £350 return, and I booked all of the internal flights separately, 1 per month until the itinerary came together. In order to justify these extravagant adventures, I understood that I had to give my 100% within the horse racing industry throughout the year.

By now I had set my sights on the higher prize, I wanted to gain a regular slot on channel 4 racing's morning line show and become a high-profile figure within the bookmaking industry, this was my goal and I was working endlessly to achieve it. I was perfecting my role more and more each day, from getting out of bed earlier than usual to attend personal training lessons with my personal trainer, to getting ready for work. I began to wear a little make-up to hide my floors, as I felt as though I was becoming the face of the business. I would do my homework on each horse racing meeting just in case I was put on the spot, such as one day at Carlisle when the news cameras approached the joint and interviewed me directly. This was no longer just a job, it was everything to me, it was my life. Rebecca was still my representing partner and we had booked a cheap get away trip to Marbella for later in the year, I had strong friendships, a loving family and a blossoming future within the horse racing industry, what could go wrong, right?

I had just returned from a long week break in Salou, and a txt from Tanya was waiting on my business mobile. "Hi James, would you be able to appear alongside me on The Morning Line show for the Northumberland Plate meeting at Newcastle next week?", I was ecstatic and could not wait to tell my Grandad the good news, this was huge for us. I asked Tanya if she would like us to have the equipment set up for the interview, however, she replied informing me it was only myself that was required. I was dumfounded by this and I didn't know how to tell my Grandad. I considered not taking the slot, however I was director and, in my opinion, a key role within my position was to promote the business and this was the promotion of a lifetime for both myself and the business, so I accepted the interview. When I informed my Grandad, he didn't seem to bothered, however I remember feeling a little unappreciated for the great lengths that I had went to for his business, but like I've said many times before "the show must go on", and so I got on with it. I began to study the Northumberland plate race endlessly, and wanted to discuss the 4 entries from local trainer Brian Ellison. I was a little nervous but the excitement quickly took over the nerves, after all I have to deal with thousands of punters each day, so talking in front of a camera about my passion was not going to be difficult. I fully intended to just be myself, I was not going to compress my personality, even though I realise that the bookmaking trade is typically a heterosexual and male dominated industry, in my opinion I was as camp as Christmas both on and off the betting stool, so that was not going to change in front of the cameras. I decided to get myself a new outfit and I wanted to feel dazzling in it. After browsing through the metro centre for hours, I went with a pair of grey tartan trousers, a pink shirt and a light blue blazer with matching dicky bow tie, all accessorized with a grey suede bowler hat, I felt full of confidence just wearing it. I could barely sleep with excitement the night before the interview, although I had already successfully completed a live feature interview at Cheltenham on Gold cup day earlier in the year, that interview took place during the betting heats, with crowds of thousands, the adrenalin aided the nerves and my Grandad was alongside me. Now, I was about to step out into the Bookmaking industry as my own person, being introduced as the showman of the betting ring.

CHAPTER 11:
"BOX OFFICE MATERIAL"

I arrived at Gosforth Park to a bare racecourse, it was 7.45am and Channel 4 racing's Morning Line show was about to go live, hosted by Alice Plunkett. Tanya performed a short run-through of the interview piece to prepare our topic of discussion, she referred to me as "Box Office Material" to her team, I was filled with adrenalin and ready to go. I began to let loose in front of the cameras, hundreds of thousands of horse racing spectators would be watching at home, I thought to myself **I need to do a shout so my punters know it's me**. Once we cut to the ad breaks, I asked if it would be ok to include my opening shout into the feature, "hea on the first event or the Northumberland plate, get em on early", I was smiling from ear to ear and I gave a cheeky wink as we closed the interview. If that wasn't enough, Tanya took me over to the studio to meet the cast and guest panellist Richard Fahey, "what de tha call you lad, yav some energy about yah", I was literally in a bubble, these racing legends are whom I study and spectate every day, yet here I was sitting alongside them for breakfast. I did not even open my phone prior to racing, I had to leave that behind and concentrate on my performance on the betting stool. Horse racing spectators nationwide and punters attending Newcastle that day would now see me as a showman of the betting ring, I felt a huge amount of pressure to live up to that title. During the day I remember the betting heats being like no other, punters were trying to climb up onto my stand to take a picture, the cameras for channel4 racing zoomed in during the betting heats, branding me as a "true showman", **this is what I've worked towards my whole life**. We attended Cartmel races the next day, which is a real country racecourse within the lakes district. I could immediately sense a following of punters wherever I attended, I was now branded as the fastest handed bookie in the country by racegoers nationwide, **I have to step up my game.**

Although I had a booked couple of long weekend brakes away during the summer, I was working flat out for the rest of the year. Tanya had txt to ask me if I would feature on the morning line again, this time for the Ayr Gold Cup meeting. This was a meeting which I had attended with my Grandad and his best pal Ricky Martin for most of my childhood years, so I immediately agreed. However, during this interview I was appearing alongside John Ivon Duke, the spokesman and promoter on behalf of William Hill. A couple of weeks before the Ayr Gold Cup 2015, the infamous steward's enquiry into the prestigious St Leger Race at Doncaster occurred, which seen the result being altered due to a collision within the final couple of furlongs between Bondi Beach and Simple Verse. I remember this being such a controversial subject at the time and Many High-profile members of the horse racing industry would be tuning into the morning line to hear the discussions regarding the steward's inquiry. Tanya had said to "study up" on the subject as it would come into our feature within the interview, I could not wait, it was like revising for an exam, it had to be perfect. The car was packed and once again the BDH (Bryan D Hazell) Team was on the road, on our way to the Ayr Gold Cup.

I had been studying the details surrounding the St. Leger steward's enquiry and i had also asked a couple of bookies their thoughts on the subject. I came to the conclusion that Nobody could judge which horse would have won the race had the collision not have occurred, so, in that instance, the first horse past the post being simple verse, should keep the race. The stewards had altered the result meaning Bondi Beach was announced as the winner after the enquiry, however the Connections of Simple Verse were appealing the enquiry with the BHA (British Horse Racing Association), this was due to be the topic of discussion on the morning line, very exciting. I was transported by Grandad to Ayr racecourse on the morning of Gold Cup Day, the sun was shining and there was a positive energy surrounding my morning. I felt nervous to be even making a comment on the subject of the St. Leger Enquiry, never mind making a statement of which horse I think should keep the race. The interview went extremely well and Once it was over both myself and John were invited to have breakfast with the team, only this time the line-up included Main Presenters of Channel4 Racing, Nick Luck and Mick Fitzgerald. I remember the look on the wee Scottish ladies face when she saw me coming in with the C4 team, this little lady had been serving me my hot drinks at Ayr Racecourse for many years, she joked "aye ya weh tha big lads naw san" and she gave me a cheeky wink, but she was right, these were the idols of the horse racing industry and I had gained myself a place at their table, it was one of the proudest mornings of my life. Nick luck approved by stating "I could of listened to you all day speaking about that enquiry, well done", they were asking me about my career direction and where I see myself in the future, in my head I was thinking **I'm not leaving me Grandad,** however I did have other aspirations that I wished to pursue, such as Big Brother, I still had hope with that, and travelling the world, my Indian adventure was just around the corner. One of the head producers said asked "can you not try your hand at X factor for Britain's Got Talent?", this set off my overactive imagination. I had achieved everything that I had set out to achieve within the industry, I was now my own person within the trade of bookmaking and very much so becoming a figure for the punters within the betting ring as the colourful, fast handed, showman nationwide. Stepping up onto the betting stool was my platform, from having the paparazzi set up their cameras in front of my pitch, to being asked constantly for selfies. I remember signing my first autograph, a woman approached our pitch at Ayr a couple of weeks after my Ayr Gold Cup appearance, "can you sign this for me" she asked handing me her race card. I was dumfounded and, looking at my grandad's facial expression, so was he, in fact, the bookies next door looked dumfounded too. She explained that she only comes racing to watch me work, and that she was thrilled at seeing me on the tele representing the bookies, so obviously I signed her race card and wished her good luck with her bet. My god I was beaming with pride.

As the weeks went by, I channelled every ounce of energy that I possessed into progressing within my career. The attention which I was receiving from punters nationwide was becoming very overwhelming, every hour of every day I became focused on becoming the best that I could be. From the second I woke my working day began, getting ready to go to the races had become an extremely time consuming exercise, I was the face of the betting ring and needed to live up to that title, from my outfit choices, to covering my blemishes with a natural facial make-up, as once I stepped up onto that betting stool I felt as though I was under a micro scope. Grandad became extremely irritated with the crowds of punters who would gather to ask me for a selfie, **what am a supposed to do,** I felt as though I couldn't win. If I refused when asked for a selfie I would be branded as being stuck up, yet if I allow them to have a photo my Grandad would get annoyed, it was getting like this every day and I was beginning to feel the strain.

After working flat out all summer the time had come for me and Rebecca to jet off to Marbella, we sat in Leeds airport with our friends sipping prosecco, **we deserve this**. A few days before we were due to leave, I was travelling to the races when I received a phone call from Tanya Steveson, " Hi James, Channel 4 Racing would like to invite you to take part in a Morning Line Special live from Ascot Champions Day next week, would you be available?", this was set to be one of the biggest Morning Line shows of the year, featuring special guests Frankie Dettori and the champion jockey of 2015 Sylvester Desouza, I immediately agreed without hesitation. This was by far my biggest achievement to date as my Grandad did not hold a position at ascot, in fact he was due to attend Catterick races that day, so to be invited by channel 4 racing as my own person, with zero links to the family business, felt a complete honour. I remember being so consumed within my ambitions that whilst in Marbella I completely isolated from the group. I would take a walk along the pier with my headphones in, day dreaming of what my life could become, **I have to give this my all**. I returned late the Thursday evening and attended Redcar races the following day. Brian Clarke collected me after racing, and we headed back to Leeds airport. I was back in the departure lounge, however this time I was boarding a business flight to London Heathrow, from planes, trains, taxis, a busy day at the races and a late flight to London, my head was spinning. I had booked to stay in a grand hotel just outside of Ascot, literally my head hit the pillow and I was out cold. I had a positive glow when I woke, somewhat from the sun in Marbs, but more so from the fact that in just over an hour time I would be walking into the Channel4 Racing studio alongside some of the greatest horse racing legends of all time, I was beaming.

CHAPTER 12: CHASING MY DREAMS

This was the first time that I had visited Ascot racecourse and by god I was in ore of it, I could feel the atmosphere at 8am with no punters or bookies in sight, I could only imagine working a busy festival meeting here. However, I was not here to step up onto the betting stool, it is one of the first times I have ever attended a racecourse without being up on the betting stool, **weird this is**. After I had presented my invitation to the racecourse security, I was shown up to the studio alongside the other high-profile names within the bookmaking industry. I immediately began to feel the pressure of being here, members of the channel 4 racing team were praising my ability on the stool "we've heard lots about you James", I honestly didn't know where to put myself. Looking around as I was sat waiting for the show to go live was so surreal, I had spent my days watching these people and idolising them from being a child. I remember queuing at York Racecourse to have my copy of Frankie Dettori's autobiography signed, and here I was being shown over to meet him in person, before sitting along sides him on the morning line, I maintained a fully professional persona whilst I was introduced. Out of the maybes 20 horse racing figures within the morning line audience that morning, only a selected few were given the chance to feature on camera, I really was not expecting to appear however, the cameras were suddenly on me and here I was discussing the feature race of the day, I don't think I took a breath during the few minutes which I spoke. Previously I had only spoken on camera alongside Tanya and a few of the production team members, however this time I was speaking in front of the whole team and some great sporting legends, I literally had a lump in my throat and I still do just thinking about that moment. I was sat alongside John Ivon Duke who I had previously met at the Ayr Gold Cup meeting, so all was well, however, to the left of me was the high profile and somewhat celebrity bookie Geoff Banks. I had previously met Geoff within the betting ring and I found him to be a little pompous, however he is still an extremely high-profile bookie all the same, so I sat and maintained a fully professional personality. Tanya had asked me to prepare some questions to put to the star guests and I desperately wanted to ask Dettori "with you being one of the greatest champion jockeys of today's era the punters at home will be lobbing on your rides today, so for those who are looking for a wager on yourself, which of your rides are you most optimistic about and why?", however, when it came to the cut Geoff banks got the air time to ask his questions, at the end of the day he was more of a figure within the industry than me so to be honest I didn't let it faze me, and I was extremely thankful for the opportunity which I had been presented with. when the morning came to an end, I thanked Tanya and the team and I made my way back into London to travel home. I had already secured a feature interview on the Cheltenham Paddy Power Gold Cup Morning line alongside Paddy Power himself, and I should have been feeling on top of the world, however I will tell it exactly how it was. I sat in Kings Cross waiting for my train home with a feeling of not belonging, I felt as though I had to maintain this extremely professional persona 24/7 and I felt as though I was no longer portraying the outgoing bubbly personality that was me. I felt as though this industry was beginning to change who I was as a person, I could not speak freely as it was either to camp or expressive, I could not speak without being mocked by pompous arseholes and I could not wear what I wanted to wear as it was "too much" or "to colourful", even my grandad began to comment on my appearance every day. "what do you want to be wearing a silk scarf for", it was comments like that, all day, every day, and I was beginning to tire of it, it was completely draining my personality, **I need a change**.

It is now coming to the end of our racing season and my work load usually begins to slow down, however the pace at which my life was moving at this time was anything but slow. A few weeks earlier I had made an application for the T.V show Britain's Got Talent, i seen this as a huge opportunity to catapult my profile nationwide as a showman. To be honest with everything that was going on around my life at this point i had completely forgotten about the application until i received a phone call, "Hi we are calling from Britain's Got Talent to confirm your audition date on the 8th of November in London to meet the producers" I remember exactly how I felt at that moment, it was almost as if it was meant to be, so I readily agreed to attend the audition and once again planned my travel to London. It was a busy Saturday race day at Kelso races and for one of the first times within my years on the betting stool I had stepped down willingly to work the computer, I had to save my voice and somehow put together a performance to secure my place on the big stage in the further rounds of the show. I had downloaded 2 backing tracks, one for Tina Turner's "Proud Mary" and the other for Chicago's "all that jazz", I know that I don't have a strong vocal ability, however, what I lacked in vocal ability I intended to fully make up with my stage presence. Again, I found myself back in the departure lounge, this time at Newcastle international airport boarding a flight to London Heathrow, my nerves were shot but the adrenaline within my body was overwhelming, I was on the biggest natural high that I had ever experienced. by now I knew London like the back of my hand, so I set out on my journey across the city to the Excel Arena where the auditions were being held. As soon as I arrived and seen the masses of people, thousands of auditionees queuing outside of the arena, I felt on cloud 9, "take everything as an experience" is what I told myself. I had been queuing for what seemed to be hours on end, eventually the crew took my section of the auditionee's outside, music was blaring and the cameras were filming. it was BGT's 10th anniversary and every act, from clowns, dancers, mimics, singers, impressionists, were out in force doing their thing, I felt as though I was in a musical. I was just being myself as I usually have my headphones in dancing away with not a care in the world anyways, only now I was alongside thousands of other like-minded people and we all shared the same energy. once the filming and queuing came to an end, we were taken into the waiting hall, it is exactly as you see on the television, lights, fancy mirrors and acts rehearsing around you, I thought to myself "my god I want this, I want this so bad!". eventually after around 10 hours of waiting my name was called, I took a quick sip of green tea and made my way to the producer's room for round 1 of my performance. as I entered it was extremely relaxed, I felt at ease and the room was quite small with 2 producers in front of me, I took out my phone and attached it to the music system set for my performance, "here goes!". Once I got myself into the stride of "all that Jazz" I was in my element, I gave my performance all the thrills and jazz hands that I could muster, I could see by the smile on the producers face that they were impressed, and once my audition was over, they handed me a pass to the next round. As I left the room my friends which I had made acquaintance with during the day were all asking me "did you get the golden ticket?", I felt euphoric, however, this was only the beginning and I was still a very long way away from the big stage audition which I had set my dreams on. I was immediately whisked away by the crew runners and placed into the hall way outside of a stage size room, this performance was set to be in front of executive producers and my nerves went to shit. I entered the room and I immediately realised the importance of this audition this was the one which I needed to shine, "just be you" I told myself. 3 producers and a camera man stood before me, I remember how bright the light was shining in my eyes as I took centre stage, "oh shit! oh shittery shit!". Somehow, I managed to get through the performance, however, I felt it went drastically, my knees were knocking with nerves. How would I manage to stand in front of thousands and a judging panel if I can't hack a room with executive producers?

As I made my way home, I told myself to put the audition day behind me, forget about it and concentrate on my upcoming feature interview on channel4 Racings Morning line show alongside Tanya and Paddy Power for the Cheltenham November Festival, **this is only the beginning**!

CHAPTER 13:
"PADDY POWER AND I" FEELING THE PRESSURE!

Leading up to the November Cheltenham Festival I remember feeling proud of the year which I had achieved my dreams, I now had one more interview to get through and a 3 day gruelling Cheltenham Festival to perform and then I was scheduled to fly from Manchester to Mumbai, India, for 3 beautiful weeks of traveling. I had literally been living out of a suitcase for the whole year, from racecourse to racecourse and country to country, seeing out my life long dreams. I had set myself a goal 5 years previous to this to backpack India and have my picture taken like princess Dianna outside of the Taj Mahal. Not only to travel India but to experience it ALONE! away from the madness that my life had become within the jungle that is the betting ring. For now, my mind was totally consumed within my career and preparations had begun for my feature interview on the Morning Line at Cheltenham.

I remember it clearly, walking onto the track on day 1 of the 3 days festival meeting feeling totally in awe of my surroundings and thinking "in a few hours this AMAZING racecourse will become chocka with punters". As usual we set up our equipment at around 10am ready for the gates opening and I began with my shouts ready for the very first punter who enters the betting ring. Before racing the bookies gather to pick their betting positions for the day from the picking list, and at Cheltenham this usually takes place right in front of our pitch, however, my Grandad holds a prominent position, number 6 in main tattersalls, meaning we are not required to stand and wait for the picking list and can immediately start betting, I must admit I LOVED shouting in the punters as the other bookies waited to take their picks, cheeky so and so that I am. As I have stated before the betting heats are like no other at Cheltenham and I have to be prepared for a silent punter to just approach me with a bag holding maybes £10,000 in it, this is what excited me the most and having now promoted myself on national television as the showman of the betting ring I was attracting the attention of major clientele and I could clearly see it! as day 1 comes to a close I would normally be heading off to a hotel outside of Cheltenham alongside my Grandad and Donna to stay for the night, however I was now leaving my grandads side and for the very first time staying at a trackside B&B ready to wake at 7am and head into the racecourse as a part of the channel4 racing morning line team, I felt on top of the world.

As I entered the track on day 2, I remember the little old security man on the top gate approaching me "excuse me sir you're not supposed to be in here at this hour, the gates are not open to bookies as of yet!", this man had been manning the top entrance gate for all the years I had been attending Cheltenham Racecourse, and once I explained to him very politely that I have special dispensation as I am appearing on the Morning line alongside Paddy Power who sponsored the whole festival he shook my hand and congratulated me, nothing beats that feeling, nothing!

as I entered the paddock and made my way over to the weigh in room steps where the camera crew and C4 racing team where positioned I remember feeling as though my mind was not fully in it this time, I had prepared a full interview spiel to talk through regarding Tony McCoy's departure from the saddle, I wanted to say "he may have hung up the silks however his legacy still stands strong within the betting ring but like everything, all good things come to an end and now the punters will look on to follow the next up and coming star within the world of horse racing and jockeys", however I just began to ramble, I don't even recall what I spoke about, don't get me wrong I was highly praised by my colleagues and by other bookies for representing the betting ring, however through-out the whole interview whilst looking into those cameras I just had my Britain's Got Talent audition spinning around in my mind. Once the interview came to a close, I shook Paddy Powers hand and gave Tanya 2 kisses (as always) on each cheek and made my way back to the betting ring to prepare myself for the spectacle event that was the feature race day, the Paddy Power Gold Cup festival. Even through-out the day I just was not with it, I maintained my full composure and actually excelled myself throughout the day, signing autographs, having selfies with punters within the betting ring and even attracting the cameras during the betting heats, I should have been feeling as clear minded as ever however it felt as though I had the weight of the world on my shoulders, "get me out of here and on that flight to India" I thought!

Once the last race of the festival was over, I downed tools, headed to the toilets and took of my suit and tie putting on my loose baggy sweat pants, a baggy top and my snap back cap, I walked back out into the betting ring and literally not one person even recognised me! "this is bliss", it was as though I held 2 identities and in fact that was the case.

My grandad took me to the airport hotel at Manchester, it was the same hotel that I had stayed in before my cruise, so I was familiar with a few of the staff members and felt totally at ease, I got out of the car, took out my 2 stone suitcase and shook my Grandad's hand "good luck son and you take care out there", I literally walked into my hotel room and started to ball out crying, "what am I doing?" I asked myself, yet here I was preparing to board the plane the next morning to Mumbai on my very lonesome.

Flying Long haul had become a norm within my life, just like the way of living in a 3rd world country had, however this felt different. Sitting looking out the airplane window and literally not knowing what tomorrow holds, I had butterflies within my stomach and as the flight left the ground, I remember feeling the stress and pressure of everyday life just lifting away. I landed in Mumbai at 1am local time, "fuck this was not the best of moves James", the streets where silent and searching for my hotel was a nightmare. I always use prepaid taxi offices at the airport so I was in no danger, however looking at my surrounds whilst passing the slums of Mumbai was simply unreal. I had booked the best of the cheapest hotels in Juhu Beach Mumbai, however, as always, I had done my research before leaving home and right across the road from my hotel lay a luxury sea front hotel right on the beach front with safety guards and a lovely relaxing swimming pool. My hotel didn't have a pool as I paid £6 a night HAHA! however I packed my backpack and toddled my way over to the luxury hotel, I gave the security guard a standing salute and wished him a well morning, he opened the door and I was welcomed with open arms into the hotel grounds. I ordered a few cocktails and food each day as I lay in my private boudoir style bed with drapes and I tipped well before I left at evening, meaning during my 6 nights stay at Juhu beach I was always welcomed into a top class hotel, then at the end of the day I would toddle back over to my cheapy hotel to get myself dolled up for the evening meal and drinks, this is how to travel!. I felt AMAZING from day one, however, one thing I did take note of was my self-condition, as soon as the stress lifted and I started to relax I broke out in spots and cold sores, almost as if my body was releasing the tention, either that or the change of countries. I was merely 2 days into my travels when I thought to myself,"I best check my email and get in touch with home and work-related matters", as soon as I opened my inbox an email was waiting from the BGT production team. "Hi James, I have been assigned as your researcher for the Britain's Got Talent series and need to speak with you urgently regarding your audition, can you give me a contact number", my phone was totally unreachable so I asked my researcher to forward me her number, my heart was beating and I could feel the excitement beginning to take over my body. As soon as my researcher sent over her number, I literally ran along the street and was asking all of the local Indians if there was a pay phone so I could phone home, however communicating was extremely difficult, "me need to speak with mama and papa in England, do you have phone?" *using my hands symbolling a telephone against my ear*, eventually after running half way down Juhu Beach I came to the bus station right at the far end where a very lovely Indian bus driver kindly allowed me to use his personal mobile phone. As the phone began to ring my heart fell out of my arse! god knows what my researcher must have thought when she seen an incoming call from India HAHA! however once she answered I explained everything and she fully understood, she immediately put me at ease and we began to discuss my future within the show, "James the Executive producers absolutely loved your energy during the audition day and would love to invite you to the live audition shows at the beginning of next year, however we still need to do some more research regarding yourself and the producers would like to see 5 Videos of you performing". My mind was going into overload, jeeeeeesus why aren't I home god damnit!! however my researcher understood how hectic my life was at home and she told me to relax and enjoy my travels and we could do the online auditions once I return home, thankfully! this allowed me time to piece together 5 performances for the next stage of the audition process. I decided on Tina Turner's "Proud Mary", Chicago's "All That Jazz", Shirley Basey's "Hey Big Spender" and Little Mix's "Little Me", I had 3 weeks to think over the performances and to rehearse, and my voice could rest from all the shouting which I had put it through whilst on the betting stool at Cheltenham! **let's do this.**

CHAPTER 14:
MY BIGGEST ADVENTURE; THE TAJ MAHAL

As I left Mumbai having fully relaxed in the Sea front hotel, taking in the breath-taking sunsets from Juhu Beach, I was fully prepped and ready for 8 nights on the road, or should I say in the air lol. I flew from Mumbai to Agra ready to achieve my goal of seeing the Taj Mahal. All my life I had arrived at airports and been badgered for taxi's, "you want taxi sir, oi dell boy, you want taxi, cheap price", so to my surprise when I arrived at Agra Airport I was not approached by a single one, as I stood feeling lost and wondering what the hell was going on, I asked one of the taxi men holding a family's pre booked taxi sign, "sir you must have a pre booked taxi! this is a military airport and NO unauthorised vehicles are allowed to enter for security, you must walk" . . . WALK ! bloody WALK! it was 2 miles to the entrance of the Airport, it was 40 degrees Celsius and one wheel had broken off my suitcase, I wish I had videos of this moment as I dragged my 2 stone broken suitcase down the dirt paths. What got me more pissed off was the couples who had pre booked taxi's just driving past me smiling out of the window as I'm drippin with sweat dragging my case behind me, not one offer of a lift, not one !!! however eventually I arrived at the entrance covered in dirt and sunburnt to hell, I passed through security on the gates and entered into Agra to what I can only describe as going back 100 years in time. it was AMAZING to experience, they still use horse and cart and monkeys were swinging freely from tree's everywhere, one thing to note about Agra is that monkeys are dangerous, never ever walk the streets whilst eating as they will come down unexpectedly to pinch your food and they will put up a fight to get it! Once I arrived to my hotel, I just wanted a beer on the roof top and to watch the world pass by below me, Agra is a non-alcoholic state however tip a little and a beer is possible. It was extremely smoggy however from the hotel roof top I could see the Taj Mahal in the distance, I was caged in on the roof top to protect me from the wild monkeys although it was amazing watching them play on the roof tops around me, an utterly breath-taking moment within my traveling years. It was an early night that night in preparation for an early morning to explore the Taj Mahal, I want to experience that excitement every day of my life if possible and inspire others to travel and feel the excitement in which I felt this evening, that is my goal in life, that is one of my reasons for writing this book! so let's get on with it.

I left early morning and I wanted to spend the day exploring not as a tourist but as a backpacker, so I deterred away from the planned tourist excursions (waste of time and money) and I went it alone. As soon as you walk out into the streets of Agra rickshaws are at your call, I would advise anyone to attract the rickshaw you like the look of and negotiate a price for that rickshaw to be your driver for the entire day, maybes a few hundred rup's at most! once I arrived at the Taj there was 2 entrances, the eastern gate and the western gate, I'm not sure which route I took, however I think they're both similar but I can say it is like a scene from Slumdog Millionaire, literally! kids running between your feet, beggars pulling on your arm or trying to sell you something, however it is actually extremely cultural to experience, it is all part of the Indian Journey. I then paid for my Ticket at the Ticket office, I paid 750 rupees for a day pass, just show them you have it and you skip the local ques as it is a mosque for the locals to prey. I paid for a professional photographer to come inside with me, he was great for 500 rupees (5 quid), he created a full album of amazing professional photographs. Once inside you come to a sort of gateway building which is Spectacular, once you make your way through the Taj gateway you immediately see the Taj Mahal in full view, the Sheer size and total awe of the spectacle that is the Taj Mahal hits you in the face, it just holds this unexplainable presence within its surroundings. I immediately asked the photographer to take me to the Princess Dianna seat to have my professional photo taken just as she did, i felt utterly amazing, like a prince but with a £5 hotel and a broken suitcase! once the photos were complete, which took about 2 hours, I then wanted to take a look inside. All that I can say is "CHEEEEESY feet"!! blur it STANK to high-heavens above, it is compulsory to go into the Taj bare footed and in that heat, it bloody stank, however all the same it was amazing! Once I was done with my time inside the Taj it was approaching evening and I wanted to experience the Taj Mahal Sunset from the other side of the river, this is a MUST do Taj experience. The sun sets to the right of the Taj as you look at it from the other side of the river, it is about 100 Rup's entrance fee and it is simply breathtakingly beautiful! the pictures and memories of this will live with me forever. That was it, I could now cross another "must see" destination off my bucket list and WOW what an experience this was.

As I departed Agra, I felt I had experienced all that I could experience and I only spent 2 days in Agra which is all I would advise. From Agra I went on to Khajuraho to explore the karma sutra temples.

I must admit once I landed in Khajuraho I felt exhausted, from Cheltenham to Mumbai to Agra and now Khajuraho, I was feeling the strains of traveling and living out of a suitcase. I could not wait to arrive in Goa to relax for 10 nights on the beach or by the swimming pool, however, for now, it was stick huts and basic nowts which is true outback country traveling at its finest and that is exactly how I would describe Khajuraho, Indian Farmers land and lots of ganga, you can smell it everywhere! I was only staying 2 nights again and I would definitely not recommend any longer, it literally consists of one dirt path with a few buildings and very few places to eat or drink, however I wanted a moped to explore the surrounding Indian country side. I had struck up a friendship on my first night here with an Indian lad about the same age as me, he invited me to eat with his family, traditionally you always eat sitting on the floor using your hands in India and it was great to experience this culture from a true Indian countryside home. The lad, who's name I have forgotten, owned a moped so off we went to explore. He took me to see all of the Khama Sutra temples and we drove into the countryside for the whole day it was amazing and I thank him for welcoming me with open arms, that's the beauty of traveling, there is a place for everyone! you never have to feel alone as there is no need to be alone, life is an open book and you fill in the pages and boy it's a big world waiting to be explored, I love to find places like Khajuraho, it truly is delving into the unknown!

The next day I set off back to Khajuraho airport, this time flying to the Captial City of India, New Delhi. I planned this as a brake up journey from Khajuraho to Goa and boy I was ready to feel the city life vibes again. I departed on a night flight and I landed at 1am in New Delhi, not the best of ideas! upon leaving the airport I was swamped by rickshaws and taxi runners trying to persuade me to book with them, I would usually always book through a pre-paid taxi office, however, it was late, the que was very long and I just wanted to get to my hotel, so I bartered the price and accepted a roadside taxi. When shown to my taxi it was a scooby doo type van and I took note of everything as I got inside, the first thing that I struck my attention was the fact that 2 men were sitting in the front of the vehicle, one Indian man driving and another in the passenger seat, However I was so tired and I had already haggled the price so I got in the back and showed them my hotel address in the City. I immediately sensed that something was not quite right, the 2 Indian men started to speak in their own language, and although I had no clue what they were talking about, I just knew that they were speaking about me and it was not good. I immediately took out my mobile phone from my backpack and pretended to call my Grandad, "Hi Grandad, I'm in the taxi and I'm on my way, I'll see you soon". I told them "I am meeting my papa in Hotel, he waiting for me", however the fact of the matter remained that I was not meeting my Grandad and I was in fact alone at 2am in one of the Biggest, most dangerous cities in the world, and I felt as though something bad was about to happen to me. My heart was beating out of my chest, "don't panic James, stay calm" I told myself as we passed through the empty streets of New Delhi. It seemed as though we had been travelling for ages and I knew by my research of my hotel that it was not such a long traveling time from the airport, my mind was spinning of what I should do and how I should deal with the situation I had gotten myself into. I had asked "how long until we arrive at the hotel?" to which they stopped the car and a "Police officer" made his way over to the vehicle. I know from my many years of travelling NEVER to deal with the local police, so I just listened intently. "ROAD CLOSED!!!!" the police officer began to shout into the car, i thought "fuck! fuck! fuck!" And I just sat in the back of the van and did not say a word. As the police officer began to walk away the 2 Indian lads explained "road closed to your hotel, we must book another hotel, we must go tourist office", although I knew this was not right, I simply nodded and agreed, those men could have told me to jump and I would have asked how high! Once we arrived to the "tourist police office", it was a little shack on the side of the road with 1 computer room and a few local Indian men were gathered, I have dealt with many tourist police offices over the years and I knew that this was not an official office, however I stepped out of the car and made my way over. In my mind I was thinking "my family won't know where I am, or who I am with", I honestly thought that this was it, something really bad, I may not make it out of this one. The Indian men took me into the computer room and rang the hotel number on my printed hotel receipt, I even spoke to a lady over the telephone who told me that the hotel was closed and "you must book another hotel", I just agreed with everything they said, putting up no arguments. Eventually, it would have been around 4 or 5am when they told me "we find hotel, 15,000 rupees for 2 nights, you must pay", this is £150 for 2 nights. At this point I knew this had been one of the infamous airport pickup scams and I was alone and if I did not pay i would have been in serious danger, so again I agreed and explained "I have no cash, I must pay at the hotel". Once they took me to the hotel, which I could only describe as a rat hole, I paid the reception, made my way to the room and locked my door. I pushed my bed against the Hotel room door and began to cry my eyes out, "how have I just managed to keep it together through that" I thought. That whole night was one of the worst travelling experiences I have ever experienced, I did not get a wink of sleep and to make it worse I can specifically remember that there was a pigeon stuck in the ventilation fan clucking away all fucking night, that is one night that I will never forget.

The next day I made it my mission to get my money back from the hotel, I knew that millions of people roamed the streets of New Delhi through a daytime, I was safe and so I decided to book myself a rickshaw driver for the day. This was a lovely Indian man who I explained the whole story to from start to finish, he explained "you very lucky man, we must go tourist police, I take you tourist police", obviously I could sense he was a genuine guy, plus it was bright and early with many tourists and locals around so I agreed and off we went. It was explained to me in full, from the moment I accepted the taxi, the police officer who told me "ROAD CLOSED", the men at the fake tourist police office and even the women on the phone who told me "hotel closed" they were all part of the scam, from start to finish and if I had begun to scream or tried to run away it would have put me in extreme danger, that is why you should never accept an off the road taxi or even travel such a country alone if you do not have the experience of how to handle yourself in every situation. The real tourist police came back to the hotel with me which was on Karol Bagh Market in the heart of New Delhi, and after they had a lengthy conversation, which I understood none of, I was given back 10,000 rupees and wished well on my travels. I tipped my rickshaw driver extremely well (maybes 1000 rupee) and I was overwhelmed, overjoyed and thankful to be out of that situation, I could not wait to get out of this city and on my flight the next morning to Goa, where I was due to stay in a lovely hotel in Calangute right near the beach.

Leaving New Delhi was the best part about the City, not only had I experienced the WORST arrival, but I also had an horrendous departure as I suffered from a serious case of Delhi Belly. This was the first time I had an upset stomach during my travels of India however, I would not wish it upon anyone, literally 24 hours of hell but eventually I was on my flight to Goa and boy I was ready for a Hotel with a pool.

When I arrived in Goa, I was fully relaxed, I had just spent the past 3 or 4 weeks travelling and living from hotel to hotel and I could not wait to unpack my suitcase for the next 11 nights and just do nothing but lie by the pool, drink beers and have fun! I was staying at the Ticlo resort in Calangute, which is a stunning hotel, amazing for value and a short walk to the beach front and also a 5 minute walk to the main party strip, Tito's lane. Since arriving in India, I had spent my travels becoming a cultural backpacker, and I now could not wait to be getting mortal as a party going tourist, dancing on tables and being free spirited, trust me Calangute can offer this. After spending just one day being daft around the pool with music playing and drinking afternoon beers, I became friends with a good few of the other guests, mostly older couples however they were the best company. I was sharing all my travelling stories from over the past 3 weeks in India, this is the best part about travelling for me, sharing each other's stories! I could not hold back my excitement about BGT and was sharing the news with my new friends within the resort, they made me aware of the Karaoke night and I immediately had my name on the list for my "All that Jazz" performance, this was my rehearsal time, a Karaoke in Ticlo resort Calangute.

Unless I bore you with stories of getting drunk, dancing on tables, watching sunsets and living carefree, there is only one main memory that sticks with me from my time in Calangute and that was the wild dogs. Unbeknown to me at the time, the wild dogs in Goa hunt in packs through the night for food and you have to be very careful not to end up alone in a dark area as they will attack. Well, here I was, finishing a night drinking grey goose on Tito's lane, I actually ended up back to a party with a group of Russians. However, when leaving their hotel at early hours in the morning and attempting to walk home I just remember hearing the growls and seeing the glaring eyes in the darkness. "SHIT!", I don't know how but I managed to run my fastest whilst being chased by these barking wild dogs, I ran into an open house which was above a shop and began to scream for help. The local Indians, or Goans as they like to be called, were literally shocked as I stood in their living space asking for help. I was in a skimpy pair of shorts and a vest with my nipples out the lot, their faces were a picture, however, like most locals in India, they were happy to help. They called me a taxi and the women went outside with brushes to "shoo" the dogs away as I refused to leave until they were gone, I swear I would have been their supper!

So, there it is, my travels of India and boy what an experience and a country that I will never forget, however now it was time for the gruelling travel home. During my India travels I had boarded 12 flights, countless taxis, trains and buses but eventually I made it home safe and sound. My mindset immediately focused on my upcoming Britain's Got Talent stage audition in London, I had to now prepare 5 videos of myself performing my tracks for the next audition stage.

CHAPTER 15:
BEHIND THE FACADE

After a couple of weeks of trying to settle myself back into my home and horse racing life, I remember feeling the struggles of adjusting back to a 1st world way of living. It felt as though I just could not get out of bed some mornings. I said to Grandad one morning "I'm sorry I just can't do this anymore, I just don't feel very well", he asked "what's up with ya, you look fine", that's the thing though, I just could not explain the feelings I was experiencing, I felt empty. I had been living at 100 miles an hour for the whole year, in fact for most of my years, and finally I had burnt out, I just can't deal with this right now. I had somehow successfully managed to pull together 4 of the 5 videos to send to my researcher with Britain's Got Talent and I was instructed "prepare yourself for the big stage but nothing is guaranteed", like everything within showbiz, it was a waiting game. Whilst putting together the performances for the videos I treat it almost as though it was my own show, speaking into the camera on my phone and even performing an outfit change between each song, I literally knew that I had to stand out in every way possible. Fact of the matter was, I had already begun writing this book and my plan was to go onto BGT, be aired to the nation as the "showman of the betting ring" and release my book at that exact time which would secure my future, however things don't always go to plan. Now, let's take you through the next few month's which would prove to be some of the hardest times I have ever had to deal with.

Christmas 2015 was approaching and I felt totally lost within myself. I had asked Grandad "please can I step down for a few months as representative and work from within the office", I simply could not deal with the crowds of thousands every day whilst trying to prepare myself for the biggest audition of my life. Of course, he agreed however, from that day forward I made a decision to go my separate way from my Grandads Business and leave the betting ring. I had my heart set on Britain's Got Talent now more than ever, it is all or nothing.

After the New year I departed the country once again, this time for 3 weeks in Thailand, with my good friend Julie. When the flight departed, I felt the whole world literally lift from my shoulder's once again, this is why I travel, it saves my life. Thailand had become a second home to me however, it was also a place where I could unleash myself without having to care. Suddenly I found myself drinking alcohol every day from morning to night, trying to contemplate everything back at home and what my next move would be. It would be during the last week of my holiday when I received the email from my researcher, "Hi James Congratulations, we would like to invite you to attend the Stage Audition at London Dominion Theatre on Saturday 23rd January 2016" . . . "OH shitery SHIT". I was due to arrive at Newcastle Airport on Friday 22nd January 2016, leaving me 1 day to prepare my outfit, arrange my backing track CD, travel to London and prepare myself to perform in front of 3000 people at the Dominion Theatre, **let's do this**.

I immediately began to put actions into place, contacting my musical friend Steph Seymour back at home to prepare the backing tracks and have them put onto a CD. I also had to contact home to prepare my outfit for the audition and book my travels to London, I remember it being so stressful but so exhilarating! I was literally lay by the swimming pool in Pattaya organising and preparing for the biggest day of my life. It would leave me a total of 14 hours from landing in Newcastle to gather everything together before departing from Newcastle on my bus to London, this is crazy!

Once we landed back at Newcastle International Airport, my best friend Claire came to collect us. I remember being so excited about the Audition, I could not stop talking about it! Claire said one thing to me which will always stick in my mind, "James I know you have done amazing to get this far and I am proud of you, however I also know what you are like and you have to prepare for the worst as well as the best!", however I was lost in a bubble at the time. Once we arrived back to my hometown of Consett I started to prepare everything ready for the audition, I managed to fit in an hour soak in a bubbly bath to try and relax me from my jetlag, however I felt far from relaxed. Suddenly I found myself back on the road again as I waited for my bus in Newcastle, all I wanted to do was sleep during my 7 hours journey to London.

CHAPTER 16:
LOST WITHIN THE BRIGHTEST LIGHTS

As I woke to the bus driving calling the final stop at London Victoria bus station I thought "this is it", it all comes down to this. It was 7am and I had only 3 hours to not only get myself ready for the Audition day, but to travel across London to the Dominion Theatre in the west end. I had my outfit in a suit bag and make up in my backpack, I had to search for the nearest McDonalds and ask the lady if I could use the disabled toilet facilities to get dressed. I explained my situation and of course I understood that I would need to allow others to use the toilet should they need to, luckily it was no problem and after about 1 hour of getting myself dressed up, I was ready to make my way to the Theatre. I was alone however, another of my best friends Josephine who lived in London offered to come with me and once running it past my researcher, she was on her way to meet me at the theatre. As I came up the escalators from the underground station directly opposite the Dominion Theatre, I could see the commotion that surrounded the Britain's Got Talent auditions, although I could have auditioned nearer home, my dream has always been to experience the brightest lights in London and here it was. Once being passed by the check in security, I was immediately whisked away to the waiting room for an afternoon of filming. Josephine had met me inside the theatre and to be honest she was a godsent, I kept saying to her over and over, "I'm so tired Jo, I don't feel up to this, I just want to do the audition now", however this was not to be the case. The filming for the audition's day is extremely long winded and extremely gruelling, usually I would Love all of that, however I was suffering severely from a 37 hours jet lag and I had not slept in a bed for 4 nights now. Somehow, I managed to plod on telling myself "it will pay off in the end". Once completing all of the filming for the different stations in the waiting room, I was again whiskey away by crew runners to the studio for my Britain's Got More Talent interview with Stephen Mulhern. I was in total awe of this man, as a child I subscribed to his magic box collection every Christmas and here I was about to do my interview piece with him! I felt completely at ease as we laughed about silly things and of course my career within the horse racing industry was a feature within the interview. I had mentioned within one of the comment boxes that I could count a grand within about 10-15 seconds (which is true) so he was putting me to the test. At the end of the interview I was again whisked back to the waiting room, at this point it was around 6pm and I was seriously beginning to feel the strain. The crew runners and all of the backstage team at BGT are amazing! they constantly brought me Hot lemon water and assured me my audition would not be too much longer, "James the Crew are loving your energy in front of the camera and would like you to continue filming before your audition", of course I agreed, however boy I was absolutely done in and even Jo could see this in me. I kept having to go to the bathroom to apply more and more makeup as I felt like utter shit. Eventually at around 11pm I was called "James Hazell where ready for you to come backstage", "this is it Jo, this is it". My nerves were to shot and I felt a mixture of emotions as I waited backstage ready to go on. In front of me was a little girl called Jasmine Elcock who I had sat with in the waiting room and boy what a talented girl she is, a great singer and Golden Buzzer act 2016 from Ant and Dec, I was overjoyed for her. I remember saying to one of the runners "OMG do I have to follow that?" lol. Once backstage, I began the interview with Ant and Dec, it was a pleasure to be meeting them both and they are literally like 2 lads who I would speak to in the pub, very much so down to earth Geordies. Now it was time to go on.

As I walked on stage a 3000 (or so) audience sat before me and the judging panel of Simon Cowell, Alesha Dixon, Amanda Holden and David Walliams, I think the first words I muttered through my microphone was "this is surreal". To be honest, once I took my position centre stage and began the interview with the judging panel I felt totally at ease, Simon mocked my tan and my age saying "you should keep away from the sun" when I told him I was only 22 years old, I also spoke a lot about my career within the bookmaking industry and my travelling life, Simon used to own horses with Ant and Dec so the conversation flew great. Now it was time to sing "I'm gunna do all that jazz from Chicago" to which Amanda let of a great cheer. The music started and as I began to sing I immediately noticed Alesha pulling out her earpiece and slam her hand on the buzzer saying "arrrh please", the buzzer literally shakes the stage and to be honest I am amazed that I managed to carry on for about 2 more minutes of the song when eventually all the judges had pressed the red buzzers. I simply said "aah well, I give it a go, never mind", but in my mind I was shattered, mentally and physically broken, I just wanted out of that theatre, I needed air! When I attempted to leave one of the crew members chased after me and convinced me to return, "we need you to complete your after-audition interview piece with Stephen Mulhern James, you've come this far, just one more hour". They assured me that I would have a private taxi escort me back to the train station as I had missed my return travel home by this point, it was almost 1am! Me being me I obviously agreed and I was again whisked off back to the BGMT studio. Once all the filming was complete Stephen told me "you seriously came across great on camera, well done". Once the whole audition day came to a close, I was escorted out of the back of the Dominion Theatre into a private taxi and dropped off at London Victoria Train station. I had missed the last train and bus home, so I had to sit and wait amongst all of the homeless and rough sleepers in Victoria Bus Station until 7am, when the first bus travelling to Newcastle arrived. During the 5 hours or so that I sat in the bus station, I began to put my whole life into context. It felt as though the world had just dropped me from a skyscraper and this was the point of impact, I knew in my mind that I was not returning to the betting ring anytime soon!

After being on the road for 5 days traveling it was a delight when my bus finally arrived in Newcastle. I had a lot of time to think over everything during my journey back and I remember feeling like I was going to cave, almost like I could predict a shitstorm coming but somehow could not divert away from it, little did I know my life would soon end up bang in the middle of a storm.

As soon as I got in the house I began to cry uncontrollably. I could not hold back the tears anymore. The house was empty and the worst part of all of this was not having anyone there to support me at that moment. I walked upstairs to my bedroom and just lashed out and I head butted a hole in the door. "Why?" I found myself asking, the fact of it is when you hit a low point it seems as though there is no way out, there is no answer to the empty feeling in your stomach, however I will say this **it always gets better,** no matter what. I began to process the past week and it hit me like a ton of bricks, this is it! I will lose my status as the showman of the betting ring and I thought I would forever be known as the dumb idiot who was rejected from Britain's Got Talent. As I write this I am actually screaming at my 22 year old self, I did not have to see this as a negative, I had already began to write this book and if I had someone to sit me down and go through it as a business point of view, I should be sitting here a very successful man, not on the verge of nothing. However, my story continues and this would be the start of a very long testing battle with life.

I made my decision to leave the Bookmaking industry and move on to something new, I had been approved a council house and I began to pack up my things. I was drinking almost every day to forget about it and to help me cope with the anxiety of dealing with this world alone. I moved out of my Grandads house whilst he was still on holiday in Thailand and I locked myself away in my house. I had suddenly gone from living life at 100 miles an hour to nothing, waking up in a morning with no schedule, no plan of what to do and no responsibilities, it was torture. After maybes a month of this, I advertised my services to other bookmakers on the AGT website to gain employment, meaning a return to the betting ring however for the first time not on my Grandads pitch. I was immediately inundated with phone calls and I accepted a block booking of meetings with BK Racing. I remember it was around the time of the Cheltenham Festival and I was sat at home watching it on the TV. This time last year I was fronting the bookies in a live feature interview with Tanya Stevenson for Channel4 Racing, and now here I was sitting with a bottle of wine trying to contemplate how my life had got to this low point. My best friend on this earth Claire, who I did not even need to ask her to be there for me as she knew I was in a bad place just because she knows me. Claire would bring me food and come to take me out of the house for the day to help take my mind off things, that is friendship and loyalty.

I took back my weekend bar job in Consett and I was preparing myself for my first shift with BK Racing at Catterick. I was so anxious and nervous as my Grandad was due to be betting at this meeting, meaning I would literally have to bet a few pitches along from him, however I had to pick myself up, I will not be beaten. When I arrived at Catterick I could barely speak to my Grandad, it just did not feel right, I had grown up since the age of 6 working within his business and here I was now competing against him with another firm. I was desperate for the money so I had to get on with it. Suddenly Bob Kirk began to give me more and more shifts within his business on racecourses all over the North East, and I began to slowly settle back into the life of the betting ring. It would be about April time when I received the phone call from Britain's Got Talent, "Hi James, Thank you for all your hard work during the audition day, the producers loved your energy and we have selected your audition piece to use during this Saturday's show, would that be ok?". Of Course, I agreed, I had worked so hard for it so I wanted something to show for my work. I was betting at Hexham races During the Saturday day time and then I was due to be working behind the bar Saturday evening. Suddenly my phone began to go crazy! I was inundated with posts on social media and when I looked online, I was featured in online magazines and TV write up's, it felt surreal. Working behind the bar that evening was hectic, everybody from my hometown wanted a selfie, however I was feeling extremely low so the attention was somewhat unwanted if I'm honest. The Tuesday after my audition was aired, I was due to work at Sedgefield Racecourse. When I arrived it was hectic, punters wanted selfies, kids wanted pictures and autographs, I didn't know where to put myself however I must admit I did feel proud as I had made all of this possible for myself. I was betting away on the stool when suddenly a man appeared in front of me, he had what looked to be a paparazzi style professional camera, he stood for maybes 20 minutes taking shots of me working. I remember thinking "just get me home", I could not deal with this right now in my life, my head was spinning. That would be the last day that I would work on the betting stool for many months.

After a couple of days of sitting in the house alone, something clicked within me, **stuff this!** This wasn't me and I was not going to just sit and waste my life away, so I began to search for new ideas. I thought to myself "I love my bar job and I am very good at it so what about hotel work". I began to search for live-in Hotel positions nationwide and eventually I came across an advert for Lochs and Glens holiday company based in Scotland. I immediately applied and to cut a long story short I gained a position within a Hotel based in Fort William. This seems perfect.

Camping on the beach for 3 weeks in Mui Ne, Vietnam. An unforgettable experience of self-discovery.

Pictured by Simon Nott to feature in tales of the betting ring, being named as the champion bet taker of the Cheltenham November festival.

On the betting stool at Carlisle.

Arriving at Agra airport, India.

I loved to embrace the culture on the streets of Mumbai.

In awe of the Vatican in Rome.

Taking in the views from the black mountains in Montenegro.

My first day as a representative for my Grandad at Ffos Las Racecourse, with Rebecca alongside me.

Surrounded by the mountains of Montenegro.

I felt alive in St.Marks Square, Venice.

Shuffling the cash for Channel 4 Racing.

I would adventure around the world alone to experience my dream destinations. The Eiffel tower, Paris.

My first Solo appearance on the Morning Line Show with Channel 4. I was known as the colourful bookie for the 2015 Northumberland Plate meeting at Newcastle Racecourse.

Introduced as the showman of the betting ring at the Cheltenham Gold cup meeting 2015.

Aboard the Ventura cruise ship around the Mediterranean.

Pictured at the Grand National 2012, this picture has been selected for many Newspaper and Magazine articles. (Photo by Alan Crowhurst via Getty Images)

I loved to pose for the photographers. (Photo by Alan Crowhurst via Getty Images)

My dream come true, the Taj Mahal.

On the betting stool, Grand National 2019! (Photo by Paul Ellis via Getty Images)

I was so excited to be on stage at the Dominion Theatre in London. Britain's Got Talent 2016.

Pictured taking control of the betting heats at the Grand National. (Photo by AFP via Getty Images)

CHAPTER 17:
LIFE IN A BACKPACK

I began to pack up my house, during the 6 months of living there I had allowed the bills to mount up, meaning I was now in utility debt which I could not afford to pay, this still lies over me to this day. However, for now, I mentally could not stay in Consett, I would have ruined my life and drank myself to death if I just sat still. I swept everything under the carpet and hit the open road with my backpack. When I arrived in Fort William, I remember how breath-taking the scenery was, the peace just seemed to flow through the air, it was pure bliss and just what I needed.

As the weeks began to pass, I could feel myself getting stronger and stronger as a person again, my drinking had reduced massively and I was concentrating on gaining experience within the hospitality industry, something I consider myself to be extremely good at. I was working 50+ hours a week, life at home and within the Bookmaking Industry was a million miles away however when a festival meeting cropped up, such as the Northumberland Plate at Newcastle, I would begin to crumble a little, thinking "how has my life came to this". It would not be too long before I became bored and irritated with life in Fort William, so once again I decided to hit the open road with my backpack. This time my move was across the Scottish Highlands to another Hotel in Pitlochry.

My life had become so unbalanced, so unsettled that it was hard to contemplate, and sometimes impossible to deal with. Although I had put myself in this situation, I would find it impossible to sleep at night with constant thoughts of "why can't I settle?". It was almost as if I had to be on the move constantly, I had to be travelling somewhere new as it was the only thing I could relate to. My whole life had been spent on the road or travelling abroad, and the whole "working 9-5" thing just was not for me, I simply could not adapt. It would only be a few months after I arrived in Pitlochry when again I upped sticks and left, however this time I planned to return home and I planned to make my return to the betting ring. This took some balls!

When I returned home, I went back to living in a box room at my Dad's and Bekki's house. My drinking had started to spiral out of control, I was drinking more now than I ever had in the past. Alcohol has always been a coping mechanism for me and I'm sure you have come to realize that I am not going to hide the fact that I have my issues, dear me, we all have issues. During my years of being a young adult, no matter how bad my drinking became, I had always received guidance from my Grandad to pull my back onto the correct tracks and to keep me focused within the Horse Racing and Bookmaking industry, however I felt that I had lost that guidance and my life was beginning to crumble in front of my eyes. I'm not going to hold back in this book, I want to share the whole truth with you, to make you all aware of the severe damage substance abuse can do to your body, mental health and way of living. In the past, many years ago, I had experimented with drugs, however when I became an adult, I was strongly against the use of drugs with the exception of a small use of cannabis. Over the years it was evidential that cocaine had become a bit of an epidemic within my hometown, all of my mates were taking cocaine on a night out, however I would always refuse, "I have a career to think of". Now, here is my 23-years-old self with no vision of a future. Waking up on a morning physically and mentally unable to get myself out of bed, drinking myself into an oblivion and eventually turning to the use of cocaine. I remember my exact thoughts when I was at my worst, "I've thrown it all away", which would always lead me to think "ah well what the hell, I've got nothing to lose now", and the cycle would continue. Sometimes I would stay out for days on end, partying from one house to the next, heavily drinking, smoking and using cocaine, I was an utter mess. From day one I have battled to stay on the right track in life and my attitude has always been "no matter how bad things get, it will always get better", so I quickly picked myself up and continued to fight for my life.

Once I had settled back into life at home and I had gotten over the initial anxiety of returning to the betting ring things began to get better. I was going out racing again, now more than ever, and my punters who always bet with me were happy to see me back on course. One of my punters Dominic, who I have mentioned earlier, was overjoyed to see me back on the stool. Him and his parents brought me a Christmas present which almost reduced me to tears as I was already extremely thankful for all of the support I had received from racegoers. The present was a large bottle of Hendricks Gin, I love my gin, a little too much, that's the problem.

Suddenly I had a grip of my life again, I had plans for the future and waking up each morning was a joy rather than a struggle. I had booked to go to Vietnam with my best friend Josephine, however I was not financially stable at the time. Josephine had been looking forward to the travel for months so she insisted on lending me the money to go with her. I took some convincing, however eventually I accepted her offer and planned for the travel just after the new year 2017. Although I was extremely excited to be traveling a new country, I also felt this sense of unease about the trip. It was almost as though I could see things were about to get bad, I really did not want to go at all.

During the New Year celebrations, I found myself excessively drinking again, even more so during the week leading up to Vietnam. I specifically remember getting myself a bottle of wine for the bus travel down to London, I was anxious about the trip before I had even arrived at the airport. As always, the long-haul flight was all inclusive refreshments meaning my flight to Vietnam was also an alcohol fuelled travel. By the time I arrived in Ho Chi Minh City, I was about mortal, however I set off to find a hostel for the night within the backpacker's quarters. Josephine was due to arrive the next day, giving me a full night alone with my drunken antics! I don't remember much about the night, just partying from bar to bar with other backpackers, the best thing about backpackers is that everyone has a story and no one will judge! The next morning, I woke with Josephine standing over me, "James cover your modesty" as she laid a towel over my naked body. I was staying in a hostel and sharing a dorm with 7 or 8 other backpackers, I had come in mortal, taken off all of my clothes and fell asleep on top of the quilts naked.

Once I woke and had breakfast with Josephine, we both began to settle in nicely. We made a few friends within our dorm and that night was lady's night in the hostel, a great excuse to put my mini shorts on and have my nails painted! Josephine does not drink as much as me, so once we had a blowout night, she was ready to move on and I could not wait to get out of the city! I had said "I just want to find a beach which is miles away from civilisation", to which the hostel owner recommended a campground beach hostel in Mui Ne called "The Long Son", it looked amazing and we immediately booked.

After a 3-hour bus journey we arrived in Mui Ne, we took the local bus and travelled around 15 miles outside of Mui Ne until we arrived at the Long Son Campground Resort. As soon as we walked into the resort I remember saying to Josephine "this is amazing", it was almost like a haven for backpackers. We had booked a tent on the beach for 3 nights, it felt as though I had travelled Asia all my years to find the Long Son!

The resort houses 150+ backpackers from all walks of life. Every night in the Long Son has a theme, from Movie night in the beach side movie room to Bar Crawl night were jeeps take everyone to Dragon Beach Club in the city. Our first night was quiz night, all of the backpackers gathered in the communal outdoor sitting area, metres away from the beach with the sounds from the ocean and we all played a general quiz whilst smoking weed and chugging beers, it was bliss!

After spending a few nights here, I did not want to leave! We had 17 nights of our trip remaining and I just wanted to stay at the Long Son resort, however I had to think of Josephine who of course wanted to travel further afield, this being her first trip to Asia. We decided to take a 5-hour bus journey up through the hills to DaLat. We hired a moped as soon as we arrived, we almost killed ourselves attempting to drive it, however once we got the hang of it, off we went adventuring through the hillsides and waterfalls. One specific place of interest in DaLat is the 100-cave bar. This is no ordinary bar; it has been built through caves deep underground. We literally ordered a drink with a few lads that we had met and adventured down into the caves. After a few nights of adventuring in DaLat, Josephine was ready to move on again, however I was not. I felt as though I needed to return to the Long Son Mui Ne! I explained to Josephine and gave her the option to come with me, however she decided to continue travelling and I returned to the Long Son Mui Ne alone.

I want to describe the Long Son resort in a bit more detail for you to appreciate how important this place was to me at this time. The resort is a haven for backpackers from all over the world. There is a bar, restaurant, movie area (set on the beach side), dorms and tents set on the beach. When at the Lon Son the turnover of backpackers is usually every 2 days, meaning you get to meet about 100 new travellers every 2/3 days. The communal sitting area, set with couches and bean bags, really is the hub for all guests to socialize. Every day the resort has an activity for guests, from Movie night, poker night, sand castle competitions and a bar crawl. The bar crawl was my favourite, everyone is picked up and transported to the Dragon Beach Club on safari jeeps. During my stay I became more like a member of staff than a guest. One day I took the challenge of arranging the bar crawl. I went around the camp ground all day with my booking form and clip board, selling out the bar crawl which is 5 dollars. It included the jeep transfer, shots, club entrance and shisha. After spending my whole day and using my persuasive persona, I managed to get 58 guests to sign up to the crawl, even the staff where shocked, but everyone was so excited. On a night I would do my own thing, just take a beer and sit on the wooden swing looking out at the sea for hours, reflecting over how much my life had changed this past year.

It was almost time to travel back home and face reality once again, this hit me so hard. I was in floods of tears and really did not want to go home, if I was in a better financial position at the time I would have stayed and worked at the Long Song, however I had work commitments and I had to face up to life. I had met 100's of amazing people from all over the world, however only a handful actually made an impact on my life. 1 person who I will never forget is Michael, he was from Germany and we connected immediately. I met Michael about 3 days before I was due to leave which made it all the more difficult to deal with. I have since lost contact with him however I would LOVE to come across him again at some point in my life. Life is mysterious in all kinds of ways, so I might just bump into him again on my travels.

"This is it, 2017 is my year" . . . Ooh how wrong could I be?

CHAPTER 18:
FUCK THIS INDUSTRY!

Once I arrived back home from Vietnam, I threw myself into my work. I remember feeling positive for the first time in months, I actually wanted to get up on a morning and make the effort. I had taken on an evening job at a local countryside pub until my horse racing bookings picked up. Our working year as Bookmakers kicks off from the eider chase at Newcastle in February. All be it the Eider Chase is a feature race day during the N.H season at Newcastle, however it had been a long time since I worked a big festival race day. By this point my Grandad had sold a lot of his festival pitches, such as Cheltenham and The Aintree Grand National, however we still had some extremely good pitches, one of which being Ayr N.H and the Scottish Grand National was fast approaching. I felt the fire in me belly arise once more, excitement planning my outfits and generally buzzing to be in front of the crowds creating immense betting heats for my grandad's business. I thought I had come through the bad times, for months now my emotions and feelings had been erratic. I allowed my alcoholism to spiral out of control, I shut myself away using alcohol as a coping mechanism. Some mornings unable to get myself out of bed with the anxiety of losing everything. My recent travel escape to Vietnam allowed me to sit back and evaluate my life, "I have everything to live for", I am not going back to that dark place in my life!

My Grandad had reinstated my representative position within the business and for the first time in years I attracted the attention of another bookmaker in GW Sports. I was booked to work every feature race day and festival meeting at York Racecourse for GW Sports, this was a big deal for me, opening the doors to build connections within the horse racing and bookmaking industry once more.

The Scottish Grand National was a great success, I had tipped the winner Vicente who had won the race in 2016. I actually tipped Vicente to win the 2017 Grand National at Aintree, however when falling in the early stages of the race I seen the Scottish National as a real target for him. Once again, I was attracting a lot of attention from both punters and Bookmakers within the betting ring nationwide. On one hand I would have a punter asking for a picture or to sign a race card, and on the other hand I would have a bookie making some sly remark about either my dress sense or just me as a person, however each night I would get into bed telling myself over and over "you can do this, don't crumble"!

The Dante meeting at York was approaching, it happened to fall on my Birthday in 2017 which i did not mind at all as I was cutting back on the alcohol as much as possible, so the distraction from my birthday with work was perfect. At the time I didn't share my good news about securing the bookings with GW sports with anyone, obviously my Grandad knew as he really set up the arrangement, however I had an overwhelming fear that if I told anyone they would attempt to ruin it for me. Looking back, it is a paranoid method of thinking, no doubt due to the mistrust within friendships and family relationships in the past and the feeling that certain people want to see me fail. I found myself reaching for alcohol, it was the only way to silence these thoughts in my head, I was tired of thinking. This was the busiest period within my working year, I was booked to work almost flat out throughout May, June and July all over the country however I could not sleep on a night for my thoughts, I was not eating through a day for tiredness and when I came in from work I hit the alcohol until I blacked out. My best friend came to pick me up from my Grandads, I was on to my 3rd bottle of red wine and in an emotional state. I sat in the passenger seat biting my sleeve compulsively crying. "what's up James, you were on top of the world last week", I literally could not be bothered to form an explanation, **no one understands**, I was screaming inside and my mind felt like a pressure cooker.

Somehow, I carried on for another month without crumbling. The first 2 meetings I worked with GW sports went extremely well and no one on the race course suspected a thing about the way I was living. I would roll in at 6am, barely able to stand, yet get myself dressed, paint on my face and work a shift in front of the roaring crowds. This could only go on for so long, I was becoming mentally and physically unstable by the day!

As I packed my case to leave for a 2-day meeting at York, I would never have predicted what would follow. It was mid-June; the sun was shining as all the bookies arrived in the bookmaker's car park outside the Knavesmire Racecourse. As planned, I met the GW Sports team outside the gates ready for day 1 of the 2-day meeting. As I was pushing the trolley loaded with equipment into the Racecourse, a high-profile Bookmaker, approached me. "I would not let you within 2 feet of my pitch, you lost me a very valuable customer", I could see other bookies looking over as I stood bewildered by the confrontation that I faced. "I'm not sure what you mean", I attempted to carry on walking into the racecourse to deter attention from the situation. "YOU, you lost me a valuable customer, you were sacked the next day", my eyes lit at the outrageous remarks being made towards me. **Just walk on James**, I thought to myself. **You cannot let yourself crumble here**! I promptly walked away to defuse the situation, I stopped and leant against the wall of the grandstand to compose myself before walking around into the betting ring. Thoughts of anger and frustration were spinning around my mind. The incident that the bookie referred to occurred a couple of years earlier. A bet had been sent through to me to me whilst I was on the betting stool at Ripon. As I remember it, the bet was each way on a horse at odds of SP (Starting Price), with the objective to shorten the SP within the betting ring. In the bookmaking industry many higher firms will pass down bets to On-Course Bookmakers with the sole objective to shorten the SP. for instance if a betting shop has a large bet from an accumulator rolling onto the final horse at odds SP, the betting shop will want to shorten the SP odds for financial gain, the only way to do this is through the Bookmakers within the SP sample On-Course. The argument I faced here was due to the fact the client simply was not happy with the overall SP return. Unfortunately, in this game not everything goes the way you want it to go. at the time, I spoke to the bookie the very next day explaining how the bet was left until the horses were arriving at the post for me to shorten a price and I openly admitted that I was only aged 21 years, with limited experience of this high-end business operation. Throughout the whole day working at York I could barely concentrate, thoughts zapping around my mind about this fucked up industry and the jungle that is the betting ring. What annoyed me the most was the fact that I had seen this bookie on several occasions after the incident at Ripon. I had attended the Paddy Power Gold Cup meeting at Cheltenham only a matter of months after the incident, however nothing was said, more than likely due to the fact I appeared on the morning line and was in a stable position within my Grandads Business. Now, here I was attempting to rebuild myself within the industry once more and the astute, high profile business man decides to stamp all over whatever is left of my upbeat persona. **Fuck this industry.**

I somehow managed to keep my posture throughout the day and I gave my all on the betting stool for GW Sports. After racing my boss gave me a lift to the train station and I said to myself "NEVER to return". I had around £600 in my pocket, I made my way to the nearest bar and began to sink my thoughts with gin, beer, shots and basically whatever was put in front of me. Suddenly I woke up in the reception of a hotel, shaking with the alcohol, trying to make sense of how I had gotten myself here. My phone and money had been stolen, or lost, however I had my bank card, so off I went again on a path of self-destruction. That night I ended up in Doncaster partying with some random people, however once the party died off reality kicked in. I slept under the bridge outside of Doncaster train station for the rest of the morning. Once I woke myself up, I made my way inside the station. I took a look at the departure board and walked onto the first train that pulled in. Kings Cross, London.

Once the alcohol began to wear off, the emotions kicked in! Here I was sitting in Leicester square with no money, no phone and I had not changed my clothes for 4 days. It was Tuesday afternoon by this point. I was supposed to be representing my Grandad at Thirsk that afternoon, **some chance of that**. I made my way to a library to use the public computer. Once I logged on and checked my social media account, I realised that I had been reported as a missing person, reality kicked in and shock followed! I immediately upped and left, making my way back to king's cross station. After an emotional plea with the conductor, he allowed me to enter the train without a ticket so that I could get home safely. **I just want my family**.

CHAPTER 19:

ISCOLATION & SELF-DESTRUCTION

Once I arrived back in my hometown, I locked myself in my house for 9 days. Only leaving to get alcohol and cigarettes from the shop opposite. My life had once again become 4 walls and alcohol; however, I was not ready to give up! I built up the courage to walk to my Grandads, I needed a few bits from my bedroom in his house and this would be an excuse to try and build whatever bridge I could to save my career. In total honesty to whoever is reading this, I went to the shop that evening, bought a cheap bottle of whiskey and in my mind, I was ready to give up. I was tired of it, my mind hurt with thinking, my body ached with the alcohol abuse and I had no more to give. Obviously, I didn't do anything stupid otherwise I couldn't write my story, however I had to find a power from inside to carry on. Whilst I was as pissed as a fart that evening, I searched for Live-in Hotel positions in Scotland, **I just need to get away**. Within hours I received a phone call from a Castle Hotel in the Cairngorms National Park offering me a live-in assistant position with an immediate start. **Here we go again**.

The hotel was a luxury Castle Hotel situated in a rural part of the cairngorms national park near Glenshee. The peace was amazing and it allowed me to gather myself once again. Very quickly I found my feet within the hotel and I used my previous hospitality experience to excell within the position. 3 weeks into my employment the owners promoted me to Duty Manager of F&B. I received my own flat adjoining the Hotel along with a brand-new apple mac book pro. My main role was to manage the exclusive bookings within the hotel. One that sticks out in my mind was a group of 30 or so surgeons and medical practitioners who had booked the castle for a James Bond themed weekend. I was in my element organizing the Gala for the Saturday evening, however I once again found myself mixing work and success with pleasure. That evening I stayed overnight in a guest's room, drinking whiskey until 8am and leaving to start a shift at midday. The alcohol progressively got worse within a short space of time, as I was locking up on an evening, I would buy myself a bottle of wine just so that I could get myself to sleep without sitting awake with my thoughts. Eventually it all became too much and my work colleagues had enough of my mood swings, so I was given my marching orders once again. This was a shock at the time, however, by now, I was used to moving around a lot. Roger, the owner of the hotel, dropped me off in Perth city centre where I got a bus through to Edinburgh. I had £1600 in my pocket with zero means of supporting myself, I had nowhere to live and practically no possessions, however I still made my way to the nearest bar, at this point I was past caring about my safety or well-being. It was the Edinburgh Fringe Festival at the time so the city was buzzing which was not good for me, I set out on another path of self-destruction.

I was travelling from hostel to hostel and staying anywhere that would have me. I had been consuming alcohol for months without giving myself a brake. Looking in the mirror I could hardly recognise myself, I did not know who I was anymore. **Who loves me? who wants to love someone like me?** these were my thoughts as I sat alone in whatever bar I fell into. Eventually, my body gave up on me, I was found passed out in a door way. I can only remember fighting to get out of the ambulance. The Royal Infirmary in Edinburgh put me under a mental health section for around 36 hours (until the alcohol had passed through my system). I was asked question after question about myself and my thinking, all the while I am screaming inside **why does nobody understand!!!** As soon as I was discharged, I made my way back to Newcastle and made contact with my family once again. My grandad came through to collect me from a hostel in Newcastle City Centre, I was a broken man!

I was sitting in the back of the car travelling home, staring out of the window, barely able to contemplate the past few months and unsure about my future. Just living seemed to be a struggle. Once the hype died down, I was living between my Grandad's house in Consett half the week and my Grandma's house in Leadgate the other half. I was back and forth to the doctors, more questions to answer, with the same thoughts in my mind, **nobody fucking understands!** I was referred for bipolar assessments, **I'm not fucking bipolar!**

I had been allocated a position within a supported housing unit called Tower House through Stonham, based in Consett. I managed to stay 1 night before calling it a day. **I don't want to be alive anymore.** I gathered what money I could get and booked a flight to Thailand. I began drinking again, vodka by the litre would have no effect on me by this point, I was just poisoning myself, as in all honesty I did not care if I died. I arrived at Newcastle Airport, still extremely pissed and stinking of alcohol, I can barely remember the flight. The next memory was being disorientated and intoxicated in the middle of Bangkok, with a limited amount of money and no clue of my direction, I was completely lost in every sense. But my mind actually began to calm as I was a thousand miles away from judgement, hatred, disloyalty and pain. Here I was in Thailand, my safe haven since being 12 years old. **I can do this; I can find myself again**.

Once the madness of the past week began to settle, reality hit me hard. This was no longer a case of breaking down at home, where I could be rescued from my own destruction through close friends and family members. I had this image of travelling to Vietnam to never return. I had fantasized about returning to the Long Son resort in Mui Ne to volunteer until my mind was capable of dealing with my home life, however again, this was not to be the case.

I was walking down Koh San road, Bangkok, when I had a flashback from the night before. I had been in one of the bustling bars performing a dance off with the DJ. I decided to go back into the bar to sit with my thoughts and watch the world go by. By this point consuming alcohol in the morning, afternoon and evening had become a norm within my life and so I ordered a few bottles of the local beer, Chang. My troubles began to float away with every bottle and I became at ease with my situation. I had started a conversation with a lad who was sitting opposite, he was waiting for his girlfriend to finish getting her hair braided. I immediately felt at ease with Ciaran as we shared our stories about our travels and once his girlfriend, eve, joined us, we all gelled really well. I immediately sensed my fantasy to volunteer in Vietnam slip away, as we planned to travel further north of Thailand to Chang Mai together.

It was so erratic; in fact, it was crazy! I had gone from feeling so alone with no sense of belonging, to suddenly joining Ciaran and Eve on an amazing adventure. We travelled on the night train from Bangkok to Chang Mai, which gave me a chance to take everything in as it was a gruelling 12-hour journey. It almost felt as though we had known each other for years. I never once opened up truly to them at the time as I did not want or need to burden them with my problems on their travels, I just wanted to forgot my whole life and live freely. We hired out a couple of moped bikes and began to adventure through the hills. The waterfalls and viewpoints within the hills of Chang Mai are breathtakingly beautiful. Initially, I had only planned to join Ciaran and Eve for 5 days in Chang Mai, however, we were so lost in our adventures that we carried on travelling further north to the town of Pai. Pai is by far my favourite destination in Thailand and, at that time, it was just what I needed. The dirt track roads filled with market stalls are tranquil and the surrounding jungle like areas are amazing, filled with hot spring, sunset canyons and Caves. We would set off in the early hours to adventure on our mopeds, not returning to the village until sunset. I never wanted this feeling to end, but more so, I didn't know how I would cope without them. We had been travelling together for almost 2 weeks and I had become so attached to Ciaran, without him I would have lost my shit completely. Without those adventures I would not have coped and my life could have ended up being in real danger. Ciaran and eve had planned to travel south, by this point my head was all over the place and I didn't want them to leave me, yet, they had no idea how much they were supporting me. We eventually decided to stick together, making our way south to the island of Koh Phi Phi.

Once we had arrived on the island, I immediately felt uneased by the party atmosphere surrounding me. Koh Phi Phi is a different world from Northern Thailand, it is filled with alcohol fuelled party going tourists. I remember saying to Ciaran **I can feel myself losing my shit here mate**, both him and Eve told me "you're an amazing person James, don't ever lose that". All of these emotions were too much, and once again I began to drink heavily. My feelings towards Ciaran had become so confused, I almost felt as though I loved him but not in a sexual way. I decided to immediately cut myself away from both of them, explaining my feelings and that I had to deal with my shit. I had gained a job at Slinkys beach bar, serving shots and dancing away the night. I knew I had to start making plans to travel home before something seriously went wrong. I have grown up in Thailand and it is not a Country to be losing your shit in.

Suddenly I came to the realisation that my funds had ran dry. I had to travel from Krabi back up to Bangkok with no money. I knew how to conduct myself with the locals, so I begged the Thai lady running the taxi desk to take me to Krabi Airport. Once again, I was on my way! . . . . Once again, I had no known destination other than London, Heathrow.

As I touched down in London an announcement came through the airplane tanoi, "Could Mr. James Hazell please make his way to the front of the aircraft immediately". At that moment every thought passed through my mind, **had something been put into my luggage? Was my family waiting at the arrivals desk? . . .** However, I was met by 4 Armed police officers, my heart sank to the pits of my stomach. "James Hazell, your family have reported you as a missing person, is everything ok", I wanted to break down and let those officers take me home, however the thought of facing my life was beyond my mental ability at the time. I explained to them that I did not wish to go home and I made my way through the passport control. Once I arrived into London City Centre, I made my way to the cheapest hostel available. To be honest at the time I was feeling upbeat, I had secured a live-in job position based in Shinfield, Reading, and I was due to start the next week. However, again, that upbeat feeling would be short lived!

After checking in to my hostel the Partying and alcohol consumption began, by now I would 100% say that I was alcohol dependent. Unlike most of the other guests, who would drink until being drunk and then go to bed, I would drink until black out, just to escape my life for a short period of time. One morning I had attempted to cook myself breakfast whilst still extremely intoxicated, the Hostel Manager warned if I was to do this again that I would be asked to leave. A few mornings later I was woken from my comatose state by the Manager, He had a good right to be annoyed, I had again passed out in the communal living area and spilt a can of lager all over the sofa. The night before, some other guests and I had consumed a lot of alcohol, as always, I stayed awake drinking until black out. Of what I can recall, I consumed 1 litre of Vodka, 1 bottle of wine and 3 cans of lager before passing out. Soon after I was woken, the situation became very heated, It became extremely aggressive very quickly. The whole morning, in fact the whole of that past month had been somewhat of a blur, so I cannot really remember how it came about, but I was once again attempting to make myself some food in the communal kitchen. I had started to drink alcohol again, wine from the bottle, it was around 9am. Suddenly I found myself in another aggressive situation with the hostel manager, we were both shouting to one another and I had made a serious threat towards him in the heat of the moment and suddenly I found myself being wrestled to the floor. I obviously made no attempt to resist. The next thing I knew a team of armed police were hauling me into the back of a police riot van. I remember thinking to myself **I'm ready now, I've had enough of life, I don't want to live like this anymore.** I told the custody sergeant clearly, **I need to go to prison,** I felt like that was the only way I would have a chance to detox myself from the alcohol to start a sober life, **I just want to be me again.** I was held in custody overnight then taken to Hendon Magistrates court for my hearing. At first, I refused the offer of a solicitor, however after some persuasion I accepted a duty solicitor to help me. I explained to her that I wanted to go to prison, I had exhausted every avenue of support within my life and even another week of this reckless behaviour could see myself or someone else in danger, I told her "I'm not a bad person, I feel ill, sick to my stomach regarding my actions, however I'm seriously unwell, please, please, help me". She explained my whole situation to the court, the circumstances prior to the incident, the seriousness of my alcohol addiction and my current mental well-being. The courts heard how the incident unfolded and took leniency towards my sentence. I was handed an 18-month custodial sentence, suspended for 12 months with an order to attend an Alcohol Treatment Rehabilitation programme for 6 months. My duty solicitor had contacted my Gran and arranged for me to go back to live with her in Leadgate. I only prayed for the will to fight this; I was ready to give it my absolute all.

The travel home is a blur, in fact the past 6 months have been one big blur within my life. I remember sitting on the bus trying to contemplate my whole existence. Once I arrived back in Consett I found it extremely difficult to settle. I found it almost impossible to stop consuming alcohol, for the first week or so it was bearable, however I know everyone in Consett and everyone knows me, this comes with invites to go out. I was attending my weekly alcohol treatment meeting and taking employment where I could. Christmas 2017 proved to be the worst Christmas to date, I was so consumed within my own troubles that I had pushed everyone away. Even though I was living with my Grandma, my situation seemed so isolated. On Christmas day I refused to leave the house, all of the family were going to my dad's for Christmas dinner, however I could not face it. All I wanted to do at that time was to drink my problems dry! I sat in the house alone all day.

CHAPTER 20:
THE ULTIMATE SURRENDER

After the festive period my spirits certainly picked up. I had gotten myself a stable job within a factory, I was enjoying living at my Grans and I even cut out the alcohol for a period. I began to go back to the Horse Racing on my weekends off, this was a huge part of my downfall to come. I had become complacent. It seems to be a pattern within my life, I work until my wits end, running before I can walk, taking on a heavy load and ultimately crumbling to the floor. In this case, I was working 60-hour weeks at the Factory and taking Racing Bookings with my Grandad on my days off, I was petrified to have free time to myself as I now understood the outcome, I was totally unmanageable. It was not to be long before my next episode of destruction amounted upon me, it all started from the day I made the decision to move out of my Grandma's house. I was earning a comfortable weekly wage and I had been in secure employment for around 4 months by this point. I decided to move into a house share in the next village of Blackhill. Almost immediately I felt the overwhelming sense of insecurity, I had gained my freedom once again and I simply could not manage it. I began to drink heavily from the day I moved, it started with wine on an evening, reckless nights out, partying for days on end and ultimately drinking Gin before and after work. I was working night shifts, 6pm to 6am, at the factory and I would come home at 6am, put the television on and sit with a bottle of gin. I had begun to swap my nights for days, almost becoming nocturnal. This was never going to last in someone else's home, I think I managed 4 weeks before I had to leave. Once again, another move, another fucked up situation to deal with, my mind went into self-destruction mode all over again. I knew that I would not survive another episode as bad as the previous year, I had no energy left to fight it, I was absolutely powerless! I had to get away from Consett again, so I booked myself a hostel on Byker Road in Newcastle. Can you imagine thinking over and over of the worst possible outcome, knowing that it could break you however feeling powerless over it, alcohol had my life under its control! By this point I was drinking morning through till night, I would go wherever I could to get alcohol, sometimes just sitting in the hostel with cans of lager, or going to the bar opposite, I would always be alone as my mind had no space left for company! I would end up walking the streets through the night, even though I had a bed in a 12-share room at the hostel, I did not want to go back there on my own, so I walked around the streets of Newcastle until the sun came up. One morning a group of people hanging the streets began to offer various drugs to me, **fuck off, Like I ain't got enough problems,** however it put my whole situation into prospective. I was on a downwards spiral, I had now exhausted all avenues of support, sitting on the streets with a bag of drugs may seem appealing 3 months from now. I was on the verge of homelessness; I had no money left and my hostel booking was running out that day. I need to make a choice; do I allow myself to become homeless? Drinking on the street and begging for money and shelter, or do I get myself into a 24/7 rehabilitation house, also known as PRISON.

It was bank holiday Sunday, I packed my bags and left them in the hostel reception. It was beaming with sunshine and Newcastle was packed. I was drinking red wine on a bench overlooking the quayside. I had 2 thoughts running through my mind, give up or fight, but the time had come and it was time to surrender entirely! One bottle after another went down, I remember seeing someone I knew from home walking along the quayside, she waved and asked if I was ok, I looked back with a blanc expression, I had no emotions left. I can only remember starting my 5th bottle of red wine, the rest of that evening is a complete black out! I woke up staring at the police cell ceiling, totally confused as to how I had gotten myself here. The week prior to this I had my bag stolen whilst drunk, which contained my 2 phones and my passport along with some other personal belongings, this was an added trigger to this episode. However here I was, in forth bank police station! The officers were lovely, they informed me that I had come into the reception with a bottle of wine and smashed it across the desk. I had been screaming **please just fucking take me away**, the officer had arranged for a mental health nurse to come in to assess me, **not again surely, I have a serious alcohol addiction, why does nobody understand**. As soon as the nurse came into my cell I broke down, I explained to her "I can't do this anymore, I have no energy or power left inside me to fight this, I want to go to prison to take me away from my life, please help me". I was still serving my 12 months suspended sentence which meant by breaking the law would result in me being sent to prison. The "paddy wagon" came to take me to Newcastle Crown Court, when I arrived, I refused the option of a duty solicitor, I was ready to make my ultimate surrender and sacrifice. I stood in front of those magistrates to bare all "I need help, I have nothing left, I will use this for what it is intended for, to be rehabilitated back into the community, please help me!", under normal circumstances I would have only been issued with an extension of my probation order for breach of license, however the magistrates issued me with a 6 months custodial sentence to serve 3 months. I thanked them as I was walking out of the court room. I was relieved and ready to give this my all!

My hangover was stinking! whilst I was being transferred to Durham Prison, I was still extremely disorientated and it never truly hit me until I was escorted through the prison gates. Once inside, life becomes a whole different world. I was checked in at the reception and taken through to the induction wing (E wing), I had spoken to one of the officers regarding my sexuality and how I was feeling anxious, so they allocated me to my own cell for the first few days. we were given some tea from the servery and taken up to our cells, I remember trying not to speak to anyone or come across camp, I almost wanted to hide the fact that I was gay, it took me right back to my younger years at school, trying to fit in. Once I was in my cell my mind began to relax, I put on the television and watched the soaps, I could have watched anything at the time just to drown out the screams and door clanging which echoed throughout the prison. I began to take everything in, for once in my life I knew that I could deal with everything on a clear mind, I had zero access to alcohol meaning I could restore the power within myself to fight, to get my life back on track. I barely slept that first night, I was playing out every scenario in my mind, how should I play this out, do I just act myself? or do I hide away. The next morning the cell door opened, "Hazell, time for exercise and association", all of the inmates receive around 2 hours of exercise and association per day, the rest of the day is spent behind your door, so I made the most of it. I would get up and jog around the yard to motivate myself, ready to tackle the day ahead. A few remarks were made towards me here and there; however, I did not find myself cowering away, I was as much of myself in there as I had been in a very long time. If one of the lads threw some banter my way, I would give some banter right back, it was only ever banter and to be honest at that very moment in time I needed someone to have a little banter with me. I have always got along very well with lads, as a youngster I always had lad mates, and even as an adult the bookmaking industry is predominantly a male dominated industry, so being in here with a load of lads was not the difficult part. I found that the hardest part of prison was knowing who to associate with, I kept my head down, only speaking to people who spoke to me and even then, I would assess their every word and movement in my mind, thinking to myself **what do they want from me**. Eventually I was moved from E wing over to B wing where I was due to stay for the rest of my sentence. I quickly settled on B wing, the first few days were tough, however I mixed with a good group of lads and we would play pool at the same pool table every day. I had got myself into a routine, waking up at 8am to attend the gym, returning back on the wing for the last 30 minutes of association and then having dinner in my pad before starting work at 2pm. I was one of the prison gardeners, meaning my afternoon was spent outdoors in the sunshine. All I wanted was to keep my head down, get through this and put something into place for my release. I was working with the DART team (Drug and Alcohol Rehabilitation Team) and attending AA meetings once a month. My DART worker, Tanya, was amazing! Although It took the best part of 2 months, she had arranged for me to go to a community rehab based in Seaham. I felt more motivation inside prison than I ever had before, I had made my surrender with almighty conviction, I had made the sacrifice and I kept telling myself **"you are not going through all of this for nothing"**. In prison I witnessed some of the most horrendous activities, a man being slashed and beat in the showers and drug use beyond any level. one of my pad mates had taken an overdose of spice, I did not know what to do, he was turning blue and had stopped breathing so I pressed the emergency buzzer yelling "code blue". Thinking back, seeing all of that has done me no harm, it is a constant reminder and motivator never to return and never to abuse alcohol again! after all, I must have some sort of self-control as no matter how many times I was offered drugs in prison, I never once caved and I am proud for seeing out my sentence completely sober! 2 Weeks before my release date I received my letter of acceptance into the rehab, I was overjoyed and counting down the hours to my release.

On the morning of my release date I sat in my cell contemplating the past 2 years of my life, **what went wrong?** Why did I make the decisions that I had made, and how had I allowed alcohol to control my life? I stood staring at the 4 walls of my cell as the prison officer collected me for release, **"never to return but to turn it all around!"**. I have known what I have needed for many years, prison allowed me to be free, free from my addiction and free from self-destruction. I have so much life inside of me, I have passion, dedication, belief, the want to achieve and, most of all, the want to help others, and so I set out on a path of recovery, cleansing my body and allowing my dreams to lead the way.

As the gates to HMP Durham opened, I was presented with 2 life choices, walk to the local pub with the other lads to celebrate our freedom, or Check myself into rehab and gain control of my life again . . . I made my surrender and chose the latter, **"I just want to be myself again"**.

I was fortunate enough to have my family waiting on the other side, others who left that day were not so lucky, it really did put everything into perspective. My dad picked me up and drove me to the rehab in Seaham. Once I checked myself into rehab, I was immediately placed under a 30 days monitoring period, this meant I was unable to do anything without supervision, in order to monitor my behaviour and any alcohol use. I was informed by my workers that if I break the rules regarding substance use, it would result in me being removed from the rehab programme with immediate effect. This was exactly what I needed, I am capable minded, I have motivation and ambition however, I completely lack self-control, so I was willing to make the sacrifice and ready to surrender my life over to the care of free the way.

CHAPTER 21:
RECOVERY; THE RISE FROM MY FALL DEFINES ME!

I was placed into a lovely house, just a few hundred metres from the seafront. The house was shared with 2 other men, who became my mentors during the 30 days induction period. I began to sit and gather up my thoughts, reflecting over the years and how I had allowed my life to get this low. Up until now my life had been a rollercoaster, filled with twists and turns and at times amazing, however, very much so a car crash waiting to happen. My younger years were robbed from beneath me, however this is something I cannot change, it is something I must accept and move on. My teenage years were filled with self-abuse through alcohol and misbehaviour, again something I cannot change. My earlier adult years were amazing, filled with freedom, gaining a sense of belonging and working endlessly towards my achievements, this is something I can treasure. My Career within the horse racing and bookmaking industry was incredible, I built myself a profile within one of the biggest sporting industries, no matter how short lived the experience, I can still praise myself for achieving my goals and I can be proud of that moment. My travelling and backpacking years, which began as a sense of freedom, freedom from my home life, freedom from judgement, freedom from the bubble which I was living in . . . travelling is the one part of my life which I do not regret, in-fact, backpacking is one of my main ambitions and driving factors within my life today, it is my get up and go. However, I have learned a lot about myself from my travelling years, **"why did I want or need to escape?"** I ask myself this question on a daily basis, and the answer is simple, I never had a home to settle, I have always travelled, my whole life has been one big travelling escapade.

I want to capture my life's worth of emotions in a single paragraph, so here goes. Dealing with "the bursting of my bubble" . . . The pain which I experienced was so intense that it hurt inside, I burnt every bridge within my career, I lost the trust within my family and friends, I struggled to take care of myself and eventually I felt as though I did not want to live. From sleeping rough or in hostels, to being sectioned on a mental health ward, to being arrested and sent to prison, "**I have no fight left in me**", and so I begged for help, "**please someone *help me***". I have concluded that my battle was a repercussion from my childhood traumas, not only that, but also from living in a world of expectation, expectation within myself and expectation from others, and through the expectation I lost the sense of appreciation, I lost appreciation for everyone and everything within my life. It is absolutely fine to accept help but never to depend on it, it is fine to enjoy life's pleasures but never to abuse on them. Should you find yourself depending on help whilst abusing on pleasures then it is time to make a change. In our rehab meetings we have a serenity pray, "grant me the serenity, to accept the things we cannot change, the courage to change the things we can and the wisdom to know the difference". I am 100% accepting the things that I cannot change; however, I now have all the courage I need to change the things I can and I have the serenity to know the difference. When life deals you lemons, make a lemon drizzle cake!

Diary to recovery - Today I celebrate 6 months sober, 6 whole moths free from alcohol and the madness which comes hand in hand. This is the proudest moment of my life to date, no matter what life throws at me, I am ready to deal with it sober minded.

The second I showed weakness; the vultures began to circle. I can accept this and let it go, **goodbye resentment**.

My Career . . . well this is far from over; this is something that I can change and I consider this to be the beginning of my career. I am finally 100% free to explore the depths of my potential, I wake up every morning with a burning desire to achieve my dreams of gaining a platform to spread a message of support to others. I dare myself to dream big and I will work harder than ever to achieve that dream.

I find myself longing for more, all day, every day, I find myself longing for more in life. So here goes, I'll take you on my journey with me.

I have written my own original song, which I will now look to record and release dedicating the track to the suicide prevention act. I wrote the track "help me" aged 17, well I wrote the first 2 verses and the chorus however the finishing verse came to me only last year. "Help me" is an empowering song, it details my struggles through life. I want to spread a message of support to every single person who is struggling today, no matter what the struggle, whether it be mental, physical, victim of abuse, depression, suicidal thoughts or not knowing who you are, I want to say this, **"please be strong, be true, remain gracious and give out support and love . . . we will help you"**. I truly believe my 17 years old self has wrote this song to support my older damaged self. This song has helped me through so many a times of suicidal thoughts, this song helped to save my life. I ask you to open up and share your problems, share them with anyone, even the man or women running your local paper shop, just ask for help.

Since beginning my journey to recovery, I have volunteered myself to speak with the local youths, sharing my experience and the serious consequences of drug and alcohol misuse. People may think my ambition is to be famous when in-fact it is quite the opposite, I would love to live my life away from civilisation, a beach shack in Vietnam would be perfect. Yes, my dream is to have a career within the showbusiness industry, however, my life ambition is to help others, **"people are dying here, kids no older than my younger brother, through mental health and substance abuse, SOMETHING MUST BE DONE"**. I always refer to my own story as a guide of "what not to do within your youth", however I also want to use my experience to bring awareness of what could be put into place to help and support the youth of today. Whilst I was a teenager, aged between 12 and 16 years old, I was arrested a total of 5 times. I was taken into a police cell, locked up overnight and released the next day with no further action, **why?** I beg to question, how is it possible to arrest a child on 5 separate occasions and not order an offer of support to prevent further damage. Mental health and substance abuse problems are becoming an epidemic within the society of today, in suicides associated with alcohol misuse men account for 80% of the victims, women for 20%, this is shocking. I desperately want to reach out to sufferers and I believe I can do this through my song, "help me".

The festive season has begun and the familiar feelings of anxiety, depression and emptiness begin to surface. Over the past few years Christmas has been exceptionally difficult for me, I begin to isolate myself and turn to alcohol to help numb the feelings of loneliness. Every year I make it through the festive period with a blurred memory and a sigh of relief, however I always struggle to see my loneliness, here I am sitting within a huge network of support and with family and friends who love me, Christmas should be a time of joy, love and laughter, however that just is not the case for me! I think back to last Christmas, 2017, and the struggle which I faced, I was completely lost with very little hope within my life. Now I sit here, full of life and very proud of facing everything that 2018 had thrown my way, I have found an amazing network of support with like-minded folk who actually want to see me do well. I have re-established a connection with my family, I have regained my ambitious outlook towards life and my dreams are as apparent as ever. I have so much that I wish to leave behind as we go into the new year, however I have so much more to be thankful for, most of all for finding faith within my recovery.

Today I received a phone call from my Grandad, He has just purchased an extremely prominent position at Aintree Racecourse and he has asked me to attend alongside him for the business debut. I felt overwhelmed to be considered after the extremely unstable year that I have experienced, and so I readily agreed. I remember feeling the sense of acknowledgement within me, it was almost as if my showmanship persona had resurfaced. I instantly began to prepare for the big day, approaching this day like I would a festival. I bought a full new outfit, which was owa dapper, and each night I would use some meditation techniques to help relieve the anxiety. During my last few shifts working within the betting ring I became overwhelmed with anxiety, the vultures had stepped out in force, some of which offering words of support to my face and then criticising me at the first opportunity. However, here I am having gotten through all of that pain, I am 6 months sober and I feel ready for this step forwards.

I arranged to meet my Grandad at Newcastle races the night before, it's funny because as soon as I stepped into the betting ring my anxiety lifted, I felt at home and I felt that I deserved the right to feel that way. During the day a few crossed words were shared and Subsequently I rejected the offer to work. After gaining the attention which I had previously gained within the industry, I would not embarrass myself as much to succumb to less than my worth, I literally felt broken and the past 6 months of dedicated hard work to rebuild myself instantly fell away.

As soon as I returned to my support network within my rehab, I subconsciously made the decision to leave and hit the road. I had put together a plan in my mind, I would take a live-in hotel employment, save up enough money to record my song "help me" and I would take it to the audition which I had arranged for next year, it seemed a very thorough, well thought-out plan, and so off I went.

CHAPTER 22:
RELAPSE TO REFORM

As soon as I was on the road, with all of my belongings in a backpack and very much so alone in the world once again, reality began to hit home. I began to experience what I can only describe as a mental argument with myself, one half of me proposing and supporting my plan and the other half of me opposing with thoughts of "this is crazy". I began to create my own stress, the anxiety which I felt was so immense that as soon as I arrived in Pitlochry, Scotland, I just wanted to return home. However, it was all too late for that, I had to attempt this with all the fight I possessed. After a few days, I began to settle in quite nicely, I was extremely able within my position of employment and I gained praise from the management team within the hotel. I tried to maintain a level of gratitude within myself, thinking back to 6 months earlier where I was being transported to Durham Prison for a crime of my own admission, thinking back to how desperate I was for someone to help me, I now had to be grateful for this opportunity of progression.

I was emptying the bottle bin from behind the bar and as I walked back to the brasserie, the soul of my shoe had caught on the pavement and came loose. I had been given permission to wear alternative footwear, however I was instructed to purchase a new pair ready for my next shift. Little did I know, but this would be the start of an extremely traumatic weekend.

It was my day off so I decided to travel into Perth to purchase some shoes, it was the weekend before Christmas and I was excited to feel the festive city vibes. I had managed to purchase some shoes in the sale and decided to pop into a bar bistro for some food. As I looked at the menu, with offers of a burger and a pint staring me in the face, my mind suddenly became overwhelmed with the urge to "just have the 1". Very quickly that 1 small error within my decision making proved to be costly, 1 pint turned to 2 and 2 turned to 5. Suddenly my funds began to dwindle and my return travel to Pitlochry seemed unlikely. My thinking and actions became extremely erratic, I would be up dancing one minute, to the bar the next, shots, shots, shots, cigarette, more shots and more dancing. My entire memory is a blackout after this, with only blotted visions of stumbling around the streets of Perth.

I opened my eyes to unfamiliar surroundings; I was lay on a single mattress on a living room floor. It was still dark outside and so I wondered what day it was, I stumbled to my feet and gathered myself together as I made my way through the hall way into a kitchen. A few complete strangers were dancing to loud music, they turned to ask if I was ok, I was totally baffled as to how I had gotten here. It was actually early hours of Sunday morning, I had been out for over 40 hours and missed my shift at the hotel, I had zero recollection of how I came to be in this random house or what had occurred within the past 24 hours. I asked for a cigarette and a glass of wine to calm me down, everyone seemed so friendly and they explained that they had met me outside of a club in Perth, my face was bleeding and I was distraught and so they took me back to their house party. "I just can't deal with this right now", I explained to them as I reached for a bottle of rum, which I had spotted on the bench top. My thought process was the same as every other thought process during a period of madness, drink as much as possible to drown out the reality of my situation. Eventually the sun had risen and I had to face reality, I had no money and I was in the middle of nowhere, somewhere between Perth and Pitlochry, and so I set off walking. I found myself walking alongside a train track hoping to somehow attract the attention of a passer-by, my mind was in a total state of shock and my body felt as though it was going to give up on me. I took out my mobile phone and realised I had received a txt message from the local police to say that I had been reported as a missing person by the hotel, I remember the feeling of relief which was soon overcome with anxiety of facing up to the battle ahead. My mobile phone began to ring, it was a PC from Perthshire police and he instructed me to walk to the nearest building or farm house within the area, I was absolutely petrified, however I followed his instructions promptly. As I approached the farm house, a lady came rushing out of her car to help me, she could clearly see how dis-stressed I was and so she assisted me inside. I could hardly speak with shock and the fact that It was minus degrees outside, I just handed her my mobile, thanked her and told her the police are coming to collect me.

As I was sitting in the back of the police car trying to make sense of the past 48 hours, I realised how stupid I had been to leave my support network, which I had fought through hell to find. I was presented with 2 options to move forward, either stay at the hotel as the management had stressed how they were willing to support me, or make the hauling move back to my support network in Seaham to work on myself further, I chose the latter. "how am I going to deal with this again", for the first time ever I was absolutely sick of this travelling lifestyle, it had become my worst nightmare.

The 2 police officers from Perthshire Police department were extremely patient and supportive through-out this whole ordeal, I cannot thank them enough. I packed up all of my belongings and hit the road, the police officers kindly transported me to Perth train station and wished me well on my journey, however this was not to be the straight forward journey one would expect.

I must have stood for almost an hour outside the train station, contemplating my future and existence within this world, "why can't I just settle". I began to feel shaky from the alcohol withdrawals, and so I humped my backpack to the nearest bar for a pint of whatever. After throwing down as much alcohol as I could manage, my worries and anxiety lifts, I become care free and all my troubles disappear within this moment, however this short-term escape is always followed by an aftermath of self-destruction. My whole memory becomes a black out, I awaken in a strange place surrounded by strangers, I stumbled to my feet only to realise it is now Christmas eve, I take one look outside to the vision of everyone buzzing with the festive vibes, "this is too fucking much for me". It is 10am and my very first thought becomes focused on purchasing a bottle, right now any mind-altering substance would suffice and so I hit the alcohol with a vengeance. I'm sitting in the train station waiting room, downing a bottle of red wine with the next bottle by my feet, a can hear my heartbeat and the pulse within my head is throbbing, I have lost my backpack somewhere within the madness, in-fact, I have lost my mind in this moment. I make my way onto the first train to Edinburgh; I have no ticket to travel however I think in my current state any conductor would look on and call for assistance to meet me off the train. My very next memory is waking up in Edinburgh Royal Infirmary Mental Hospital with 2 police officers watching over me as though I'm some escape prisoner. The police had been contacted in Edinburgh by a member of the public, I had been in an emotional state of despair, crying out that I wanted to end my life. Although my memory is a black out, I can well imagine myself screaming for help!

The whole assessment process with the mental health team was, in my opinion, absurdly handled. I felt as though I was a case study who was being ticked off the checklist on the paperwork. I waited almost 12 hours before a single member of the mental health team would speak with me on a one-to-one basis, this being due to my alcohol consumption, however as I've quoted earlier, 80% of male suicides are alcohol related. My argument here is not a personal attack against the mental health team, I am not "qualified" to make such a judgement, however, it is more an observation from within the biggest supportive network in the U.K, a network that we must improve due to the severe increase in suicides. I'm sure by now you will have realised that my mental state can be some-what erratic at times, even-more-so whilst under the influence of alcohol, however as

I portrait my darkest moments I try to capture the exact emotions which I felt at that time. I am totally lost; I have no money and my mental state is so far removed from sane that I have become a complete wreck. I have found myself in a mental hospital with zero recollection as to how I have come to be there, I have lost all of my property and my face is severely injured from a fall. I have been reported by several members of the public to have been crying out for help and expressing my thoughts on taking my own life within this moment of despair. Yet here I am sitting in a room with 2 police officers, who are not trained to deal with this sort of behaviour as it is not their sector, and the only time a support worker even looks at me is to put an alcohol test into my mouth. I truly feel like screaming, in-fact I did begin to scream after sitting for a few hours, I was ready to punch my way through the walls as it was driving me further into a state of despair. After 12 hours of sitting in a room of complete silence, feeling as though I was under arrest, I was finally assessed. I was assisted into a room and positioned on one side of the counter, 2 female support workers entered through a door and positioned themselves on the other side of the counter, approximately 2 metres away. They each sat upright with a clipboard in hand, "ok James, we are ready to begin the assessment now", I was thinking "this is crazy", these situations are a case of life or death, with most cases ending in tragedy, yet 2 random ladies are looking at me through interrogating eyes whilst instructing "ok we are ready", what is this all about? However, on they continued! Each lady quizzed me with a selection of pre-constructed questions regarding my mental state, then after around 30 minutes they concluded, "we have completed the assessment and we have decided you are now fit to leave our care; we hope you get the help that you need". The police officers (which by now where the 3rd pair to sit in with me) took me to the main hospital entrance and left me on my way, it was Christmas morning, 25/12/2018, and it was minus degrees outside. I had a holy t-shirt on and a pair of ripped jeans, I had not eaten for 2 days and I had consumed very little liquids other than alcohol in the past week, yet I was just set off on my way. I am not saying the world should come to a stand-still for every person who is experiencing a mental breakdown, however suicide is an epidemic which we are facing and there is not enough action and support in place to deal with it. I can only speak on my own experiences, but let's just say someone had taken me into a cosy room, assured me everything was ok and not to worry, perhaps brought me a cup of tea and simply said "when you are ready to talk, we'll talk", then I may not have experienced the worst 12 hours of mental torture, so bad that I would never wish to endure it again in my life. I just wanted to get back into the community support network in Seaham.

I found myself wandering around the streets of Edinburgh on Christmas morning, alone and scared that I may spend the next few nights sleeping rough. I instantly began to think about my support network within "free the way" and how all of the community and charity-based support networks aim to bring the community together, especially at Christmas time, this method of thinking directed me to look for street-help teams in Edinburgh. After around 5 hours of walking the streets I came across the Edinburgh street help crisis building, which offers support, shelter, food, toiletries and internet to those in need. As soon as I entered the building, looking some-what exhausted, the whole team aided me with assistance, firstly by fetching a lovely hot cup of tea and sitting me down amongst others, I instantly felt at ease and my anxiety began to lift. After explaining my situation to one of the lovely community support workers, she assured me not to worry and that she would make it her priority to assist my travel back to Newcastle. It took the lady approximately 30 minutes to return with a bus ticket leaving at 2pm that same afternoon, she handed me the ticket and simply said "we are always here and we are always happy to help", this act of kindness blew me away, it totally restored my faith in humanity once more. I had explained to the community support worker of the gruelling, timely, methodical and uncaring assessment procedure which I had experienced through the government support network, I explained how I was held under police supervision within the mental hospital for 12 hours until I was released at 6am Christmas morning and left to my own devices, with no phone, money or public transport immediately available. She explained that I was not the first and I certainly will not be the last to experience this sort of treatment, she went on to explain that this is a problem within society, if someone does not meet the required criteria then they are simply put out onto the streets. Luckily, I was not homeless, however, without the assistance of the street help team I would have been left to fend for myself miles away from my network of support.

As I sat on the bus travelling back to Newcastle my mind began to settle and I once again started to evaluate my plan moving forward. I had immediately been accepted back into free the way rehab and supported living, I was returning to a huge network of support which I had battled through years of chaos to find, and when looking at my current situation through conscious eyes, I actually wasn't too bad off. I asked myself in that moment what do I want most from my life, aside from the big dreams, the adventurous travelling and finding love, I most want to help others who are finding it impossible to deal with life, those who cannot seem to settle into living within everyday society, and so that is exactly what I am going to do! I am going to continue working on myself so that I can be of service and support to others, through this book and my experience, through my music and through my being, I will dedicate myself to helping those in need.

Since returning back to my support network I have continued to progress every day, telling myself I am worth all of this time and effort! I sit here 2 months sober, and after the Christmas relapse I am not looking back, however I am not saying "never". I tell myself everyday "just for today I am not drinking alcohol, because I am worth more than that", and if I continue to live by that method of thinking, it tells me that I won't drink again. I live by 4 rules which I apply to my everyday living; complete at least one act of kindness for yourself, one act of kindness for someone else, one act of love and one act of progression, always remain gracious and never give up. Living by these principles has proven that my life begins to form a path which is leading me into the direction I have always longed for in life. I have an audition in 2 weeks with a talent agency whom are seeking out singers, dancers, actors and models, this could lead to further development within my life should the audition goes well, however even if the audition is a failure, I will grow from the experience and continue with my auditions. My hope is pinned on getting myself recognised to gain a platform of advertisement ready for the release of this book, from that I will then look to record my Original track "help me", which truly is a track for you. I have already decided upon a recording studio based in Gateshead, I will work with producers and musicians within the studio to come up with the correct backing music for the track, I am ever the perfectionist and I want the backing track to be created from a live blend of instruments. I have a vision in my mind for the music video, I really want to capture the audience within the lyrics and emotions and this must be portraited on screen. I am passionate, dedicated, ambitious and set on achieving my goals, no matter how far away they may seem. I am currently sitting in a box room and I share a recovery house with 2 other men, I have 40 hours of structure per week, I attend 4 anonymous recovery meetings per week and I currently live off my benefit payment of £300 per calendar month, some may say "son your dreams are a million miles away", however I have never felt closer to achieving them than I do now. I can see a vision within my mind so clearly that it almost feels real, however it is going to take immense amounts of dedicated graft to achieve everything I want to achieve.

THE LAST CHAPTER: THE CLOSING CREDITS

I feel that I have reached a peak within writing this book, and with that I feel it is time to wrap up this chapter of my life. 3 years ago, I decided to leave the horse racing industry and I walked away from everything I knew, in hope of finding myself and working out what I truly want from my life, and thanks to this book I have been able to find my best self and I will always inspire to be the best James possible. I remember locking myself away and struggling to understand why I couldn't manage within everyday society, and so I decided to begin writing out my life to gain a sense of understanding my mind. Over the past 3 years I have faced a gruelling battle with life, taking my chaotic lifestyle to new extremes and experiencing the worst episodes of depression imaginable, I have become lost then found and then lost again. I have screamed for help and screamed to be left alone, I have cried for love and I have isolated myself from reality, I have run away to the other side of the world in fear and I have found new levels of personal growth within my darkest times. I have been detained under mental health supervision; I have been locked away through a personal admission into prison, and I have fought through it all to find a support network which works for me. Thank you.

This is the final page guys, the closing credits some may say. A lot of people who bring negativity to your life will make the same remarks to keep you from achieving. The main remark for me is "James, stop trying to be someone you're not", my response to this is "have you ever considered that I am trying to be someone that I am", and with that I thank you for reading my book, you have been a part of my journey and I only hope that I can be a part of yours. A book of "new beginnings", detailing "experience, strength and hope", may well follow.

Should you wish to follow my journey or contact my management please come share my experiences.

Follow me on Twitter and see me tweeting: @jameshazell22
Follow me on Instagram and see my photos: @jameshazell93
Email my management: jameshazellmanagement@outlook.com

Lightning Source UK Ltd.
Milton Keynes UK
UKHW050611080223
416654UK00002B/101